...Hell Behind Prison Walls...

Shams, Charades & Circus
From 25 Years of Instructing Inmates

By

John J. Pecchio

BP

Hell Behind Prison Walls
Shams, Charades & Circus
From 25 Years of Instructing Inmates

Non-Fiction

by

John J. Pecchio

First Edition copyright January 17, 1999
Corrected Edition copyright August 21, 2000
Final Edition copyright 2003

Published by:
Brundage Publishing
74 Front Street
Binghamton, NY 13905

Jacket design by Nate Rogers
Inspiration by John Peccho

Library of Congress
Control Number: 2002117423

ISBN Number: 1-892451-08-5

Printed in the United States of America

Preface

According to the 1996 Edition of the *Encyclopedia of American Prisons*, the incarceration rate in the United States is now among the highest in the world and crime remains a major social and political issue.

These facts raise serious questions about the root causes for them.

What is wrong with the prison system today?

What was right about the prison system in 1900?

Is the decline and destruction of personal disciplines in our society today reflected in our prisons?

Is excessive preferential interpretation of First Amendment rights destroying the stability of our society and the stable rehabilitation of prisoners?

Is individual abuse of freedoms, anarchy against group freedom and stability?

According to the 24th Yearbook of the New York State Reformatory at Elmira, NY, for the fiscal year ending September 30, 1899 recidivism for prisoners was 14.9%.

Mr. Zebulon Brockway became the First Superintendent of the Elmira Reformatory in 1876 and served until 1900. He instituted military training for prisoners. In later years all military training for prisoners was abolished.

According to recently published records cited in this author's book recidivism for major crimes in 1994 averaged about 65%. Those with fifteen prior arrests had 82% recidivism.

Hell Behind Prison Walls author John Pecchio tells you what it's like in today's prisons and what he recommends should be done.

Table of Contents

Appendix of Pictures

DEDICATION

I DEDICATE THIS BOOK TO MY FAMILY,
WITHOUT WHOM I WOULD NEVER HAVE GOTTEN
THIS FAR

John Pecchio is 64 years old and retired. He lives
beside a small lake in Troy, Pennsylvania with his
lovely wife Pamela. They have four children,
Lucy, John Jr., Connie and Yvonne, who are now
pursuing their own careers. Born in Elmira, New York,
he worked at the Elmira Correctional Facility's All-
Male Maximum Security Prison for twenty-five years.

CHAPTER 1

AT THE CROSSROADS

"I will never go into that hell-hole again," said Jim Marcello. "I was so frightened of the inmates with their killer looks I became upset and passed out from nerves when I got home...I will never go back to that prison." Jim was hired as a shoemaking instructor at what was then called the Elmira Reformatory. He quit after one day. Jim knew I was looking for extra work to support my family. He suggested that I could apply for the job if I was interested.

Jim had quickly assessed the prison scene. Shoemakers constantly deal with personalities. Shoes must match the personalities of the wearer. They are a part of a person's personal and professional image.

We shoemakers quickly become keen observers of persons and we assess the whole person. To build a good foundation you must know the whole building. Jim had met the personnel within the prison first-hand and, coming from a fellow shoemaker, his comments were unsettling. I decided to give it some thought, but circumstances caught up with me.

I received a call in June of 1966 from Mr. Paul Doan, Director of Education at the prison, asking me if I wanted to work for the summer. I was undecided, but the same day I received another call from Doan to say that the job was mine for the summer if I wanted it and I accepted the position. I was thirty-one years old.

My reasons for accepting were simple: I needed more money to support my rapidly growing family. I now had a wife and three children. Before I accepted the prison shoemaking position I worked in Waverly, New York for ten years, operating my own business as a shoemaker. Prior to that, I worked three years as an apprentice for a shoemaker, Mr. Jimmy Stepanian in Elmira, New York. I loved the work. I was fascinated with transforming leather into useful products. It seemed to calm me down. However, in the little-known town of Waverly, New York, with only a few thousand people, business was always slow. I had already taken on a second job at the Kennedy Valve Company in Elmira, but with a growing family I still needed more work. I had also learned about the benefits of the prison job. It included good pay, good insurance for family and self, and the state would pay for all the college courses they would require of me.

Circumstance and fate move all of us. I was now a shoemaker about to teach my trade to prisoners. But my life might have been entirely different.

During my four years of high school at the Elmira Free Academy my passion was baseball. I worked after school and weekends at a ballpark as a clubhouse worker and batboy for the Elmira Pioneers baseball club. The club was run by the Brooklyn Dodgers organization. I learned so much more about baseball

2

from the Elmira players class "A" team, most of whom went on to become major leagues ballplayers. With this, plus the help of my wonderful coach, Mr. Bill Wipfler at the Elmira Free Academy High School, I became a good ball player.

At one of the baseball games for the Elmira Pioneers I noticed a tall, well-dressed man standing in front of the Pioneer's clubhouse, where the ballplayers go before and after the baseball games. As I was about to enter the clubhouse this man introduced himself, and to the best of my knowledge his name was Mr. Frank Doolittle. As our conversation got underway I found his knowledge of baseball very helpful. He worked another job, and in his leisure time he would go around to ballgames and look for ballplayers. He was employed as a birddog for the Brooklyn Dodgers (A birddog is one step below a baseball scout).

He told me, "I've been watching you play ball for a couple of years now and wanted to talk to you. You're a good ballplayer. You have a good future in baseball and I hope you continue." I thanked him when our conversation ended and he walked away. I then remembered seeing him at some of my high school baseball games.

In the last game of my senior year in high school baseball, I had noticed Mr. Doolittle sitting in the stands watching the game. I had four hits that day and ended the season with a batting average of .371. I was chosen for the first string All-STC (All-Southern Tier Conference), Honors First Baseman.

Mr. Doolittle approached me after the Pioneers game and asked, "Where do you play baseball in the summer?" I told him and about a week later I was playing in the summer league with local ballplayers in Elmira. I hit four home runs that day. At the end of the game Mr. Doolittle came over to me and invited me to go to spring training in Florida. My part-time job in an auto store gave me three weeks leave and I left for the Dodgers training camp.

Training camps usually last about four to six weeks. I was there four weeks when my brother, Anthony, who also lived in Florida became ill and was dying of cancer. My mother had eight children. My father died when I was two years old and my oldest brother Anthony became my substitute father and my hero.

He would hobble to the training field, hoping to see me play. He was so frail and weak that I would go to his home and sit up all night with him. I was worn out and devastated by his condition. Yet, out of the one hundred and fifty recruits sent for tryouts with the Dodgers, two other players and myself survived. However, by then I had left the Dodgers' camp and got a job in a grocery store to help support my brother and his family.

Four months later, Anthony died and I came back to Elmira where he was buried in his hometown. My mother had worked three jobs all her life and had received public assistance to raise her large family. I was the youngest son and the only one left at home. She needed help so I got a job and stayed in New York to help support her.

I was now about nineteen years old and again at an Elmira Pioneers ballgame I met a "birddog" for the Yankee team, the Binghamton Triplets. He signed me for tryouts with the Yankee Triplet Team in Binghamton, New York.

Out of the 178 recruits at the Triplet Camp I was one of the few left. I was told to go home and they would call me. I did not hear from them and thought that they had turned me down. A few months later I saw one of their agents down front at a local ballgame. I went down and spoke to him. He told me that there had been a fire that destroyed all of their records. Perhaps that explains why they had not gotten in touch with me.

By this time I was regularly dating, considering marriage and had a regular job. I thought no one was interested in signing me for baseball and did not pursue it further.

Now, ten years later, I was a shoemaker about to be introduced to the inside of the state prison system.

PECCHIO TAKES A THROW AT FIRST BASE

SCRAMBLING BACK—Edison's Ray Denne scrambled back to first safely in an early inning of yesterday's game with Elmira Free Academy at the Heights. First baseman John Pecchio took the throw from pitcher John Maher. The Academy won a non-league thriller, 6-4, in nine innings. (Photo by Peggy Gallagher)

Pecchio Hits 4 Homers in Midget Game

John Pecchio belted four home runs to pace Kiwanis to a 34-7 route of the Giants in a Midget League game Thursday.

Pecchio this past spring was reserve first baseman at Elmira Academy and has been bat boy for the Elmira Pioneers for the past two years.

Besides Pecchio, other Kiwanis homers were hit by John Maher, Mitchell and Johnson.

In other games Eastside outlasted Keefe's 18-11, Pennsy Y trimmed PBA 16-7 and Hagerman's downed Southside Businessmen 14-8 behind Scott Steiner's three-hit pitching.

```
Kiwanis ...  656 233 9—34 22  3
Giants  .....  202 101 1— 7 13  2
```

```
Businessmen  210 050 0— 8  3  9
Hagerman's   300 605 x—14  8  2
```
Cobb and Drake; Steiner and Evans.

```
Pennsy Y  201 10(10) 2—16  4  2
PBA  ......  020 112 1— 7  3  5
```
Twist and Carmer; Haskins and Wilber.
Hrs.—McDermitt, Pennsy Y.

```
Keefe's  ...  205 211 0—11 10  3
Eastside ...  181 262 x—18 15  2
```
Mann and Farley; Tice, Bellinger and Johnson.
Hrs.—Tice, Eastside; Van Ness 2, Palmieri, Keefe's.

Academy Romps to 16-4 Win

Pecchio's 4 Hits Spark EFA Attack

Elmira Academy warmed up for its big intracity game with Southside Monday with a "batting practice," 16-4 trimming of Vestal Saturday afternoon at Vestal.

Coach Bill Winfler's Blue Devils slammed 20 hits with John Pecchio leading the way with a homer and three singles to knock home five runners.

Bill Stamp continued on his batting rampage with a trio of hits to boost his batting average to .550. Chuck Prettyman and Jim Sampsell also collected three hits each.

Pecchio

Dan Johnson went all the way for the Blue Devils to post his second straight victory as the EFAs chalked up victory No. 5 for the season.

Academy	ab	r	h	Vestal	ab	r	h
Stamp.2b	6	2	3	Bet'c'rt.2b	4	1	1
Holmes.cf	6	1	2	Carg'l.lf-p	3	2	2
Pariso.3b	5	1	1	G.Hill.ss	4	0	2
Pr'tym'n.rf	5	2	3	Grannis.c	4	0	1
Sampsell.c	5	3	3	Bailey.rf	2	0	0
Pecchio.1b	5	2	4	Mann'g.cf	0	0	0
Mitchell.lf	5	2	2	Stanton.cf	3	0	0
Claire.ss	5	2	1	J.Hill.1b	3	1	1
Johnson.p	4	1	2	O'Hara.3b	3	0	0
				Kuenzli.p	0	0	0
				Terry.p lf	3	0	1

```
TOTALS   46 16 21   TOTALS  29  4  8
Academy .................. 131 365 4—16
Vestal ................... 101 200 0— 4
```
RBI—Stamp 2, Holmes 3, Pariso 2, Prettyman 1, Sampsell 1, Pecchio 5, Claire 1, Johnson 1, Bettencort 1, Cargill 2, Bailey 1. 2-BH—Holmes, Sampsell, Prettyman. HR—Pariso, Pecchio, Cargill. BOB—Johnson 1, Cargill 1. SO—Johnson 2, Terry 3, Cargill 1. LOB—EFA 10, Vestal 4. WP—Terry. Balk—Cargill. HBP—By Johnson (Bailey). DP—Claire-Pecchio. W—Johnson (2-0). L—Terry.

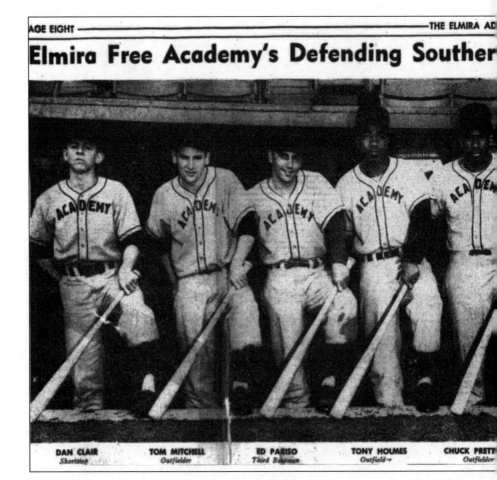

AGE EIGHT ── THE ELMIRA AD

Elmira Free Academy's Defending Souther

| DAN CLAIR | TOM MITCHELL | ED PARISO | TONY HOLMES | CHUCK PRETT |
| Shortstop | Outfielder | Third Baseman | Outfield | Outfielder |

Courtesy of *the Elmira Advertiser*

RTISER————————————————————MONDAY, MAY 14, 195

Tier Conference Baseball Champions

AN	JOHN MAHER	JOHN PECCHIO	MIKE STANSFIELD	JIM SAMPSELL
	Pitcher	*First Baseman*	*Outfielder*	*Catcher*

ACADEMY CHAMPS

ACADEMY'S CHAMPS—Although the Elmira Academy baseball team lost the inter-division playoff to Binghamton North Saturday, 5-4, it still finished with the best record an EFA team has ever had. In all, 15 games were won, 3 lost. First row: Doug French, Bill Reed, Ernie Davis, Dan Johnson and Al Howland. Bob Gush, Tom Mitchell, Bill Stamp, Danny Claire and Ed Pariso. Second row: Coach Bill Wipfler, Stan Youmans, Mike Stansfield, Jim Sampsell, John Pecchio, Chuck Prettyman, and manager Dick Davis. Third row: John Maher, Tony Holmes, Rusty Hood, John Johnson and Al Howland.

CHAPTER 2

A BRIEF HISTORY OF PRISONS

The history of the prison system dates back to the 16th Century where the applied concept meant "Lawful Detainment." Prisoners were contained to dungeons and other quarters less definable for indeterminate periods. During incarceration prisoners were either used as slaves to perform manual labor or other wishes that those in power might decide, or expediently executed without hearings.

As one might imagine, pardons were rare. "Rehabilitation" in terms of education or vocational training was a term waiting for another three centuries to be defined. A prisoner did not have a say as to his medical treatment or his meals. He had to accept what the prison provided and there was no legal permission granted of any sort to seek appeal for a reduction or dismissal of his sentence.

Punishment for crimes during the American colonial times usually involved placing the offender in stockades, leg irons and chains fastened to his legs and wrists. Other forms of punishment were public whippings, cropping of ears, exile or even execution by hanging in the public square. A new twist was added when the colonies secured independence from England, where a new authority from the traditional doctrines of liberty and faith in universal progress included a prison system with a rudimentary code of ethics.

The first prison in the state of New York was built in Newgate. Unlike Auburn and Sing-Sing which followed, Newgate planted no seeds for a correctional future and was nothing more than a "containment center." Newgate was designed for fewer than four hundred and fifty inmates in 1787, the concept remaining in place for only thirty-one years. It was eventually replaced by Sing-Sing in 1818.

In March 1796 a law was passed creating a schedule of punishments for crimes committed. Only treason and murder were considered capital offenses under this updated mandate. Other crimes formerly punishable by death were considered situations calling for life imprisonment. Periods of confinement were calculated very exactly depending upon the severity of the crimes. Time served in a county jail involved one year or less, while extended sentences were served in the state prisons.

The system was not without its problems. A rapid population growth in New York City coupled with the return of soldiers from the War of 1812 set the stage for a booming crime wave. Conviction doubled in 1815 and seemingly overnight Newgate was bulging at the seams with offenders. As could be imagined, inmates were crammed into every available space or released by pardons—a result of a "good time law" passed in 1817, which permitted inspectors to shorten an inmate's stay by a full one-quarter. Not a "true fix" by any means, Newgate's future was predictable and this inevitability led to Sing-Sing's rise in 1818.

Time passed, the legal system grew and eventually the "rights" of those incarcerated became a big deal. The prisoners of yesterday are no more.

Mr. Zebulon Brockway was the Superintendent of the Elmira Reformatory from 1876–1900. He is reviewing a military-style drill of prisoners, marching with wooden rifles, in June of 1885. This was a good form of discipline, but it was later abolished.

Military-Dress Parade—prisoners are dressed in full uniform at the Elmira Reformatory courtyard in the early 1900s. This was an excellent form of discipline that was stopped by prison leaders.

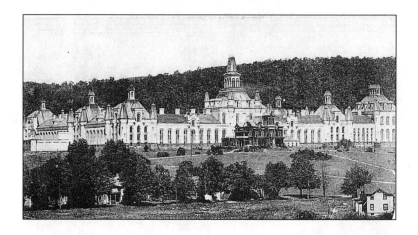

This picture dates back to the 1900s when the prison was called the Elmira Reformatory. About 50 years later the name was changed to the Elmira Correctional Facility and Reception Center. The structure stayed the same, but it has since been renovated. At the time the superintendent's house was located in front of the prison, off the prison's main door, located in the middle of the picture.

CHAPTER 3

INTRODUCTION TO PRISON LIFE

I admit I did not really know what I was getting into. I had lived in Elmira all my life and passed the prison many times. It was a beautiful building perched on a large hill. From the outside it looked peaceful. Earlier I was on a baseball team that was invited to play the inmates in a game. That was my first good look at the inside of the prison. It was just like a city of its own; inside was another world I was not sure I was ready to enter.

After accepting the job I soon established a three-job workload. My work life started to fall into a schedule. I would work in the factory full-time on the night shifts, in the prison during the day and in my own shoemaking shop on the weekends.

I began my job at the Elmira Reformatory on June 21, 1966. That morning at 9:00 I was to meet Lieutenant Warner, a veteran of twenty years service in reformatories within the state. He would introduce me to the vocational instructor with whom I would be working and take me on a tour of the prison.

We began our tour walking through four heavy steel doors, each one locking behind us as we exited. When the last door opened we entered a large yard, the size of two football fields where approximately two hundred and fifty inmates stood around. Mingled voices were audible, but there did not seem to be any interaction between the inmates. It was almost like the sound of angry insects buzzing. I wondered about my decision.

"Be careful and watch your back," said Warner. "These guys are restless and anything can set them off in the wrong direction." I felt uneasy and was quite relieved when we finally reached the end of the yard where a tall steel gate opened ahead of us. It opened into the center of the prison compound.

"This is Center Gate," Warner said. "It's where all personnel enter the work area." A guard locked inside a small booth near the gate operated the controls and received any emergency calls which in turn set alarms off, thus controlling the entire prison. To me, it seemed to be a complicated arrangement and my discomfort increased since we were surrounded by inmates until the gate opened, and permitted us to walk on through.

Other vocational shops, including a hospital, schools, and a foundry, were located on two separate floors in seven different buildings. The rooms were open areas without bars or screens to contain or separate the occupants from each other or from the instructors. Also inside this large inner area there was a ballpark, a swimming pool, and an armory where inmates gathered during recreation periods.

We finally reached the shoemaking shop where I would be working. There were about thirty inmates in the room and the sound of machinery created a busy atmosphere. The smell of leather made me feel at home and eased the tension I had been feeling. Warner introduced me to my supervisor, Joe Bono, who was standing in the doorway of the office, talking to Harold Cooper, the instructor. Seeing us enter the room Bono came forward to greet us. His raspy voice was one that I would hear in the future many times, often when I would rather not listen to it.

As we were talking, Harold Cooper stepped out of his office to meet me and Warner introduced us. I was his replacement for the summer vacation. Cooper was a tall heavy-set man about sixty years old. His penetrating look made me feel like he had gotten inside my head and evaluated my brain.

"I'll show you the ropes for the next couple of days, and then you're on your own. I'm leaving for my vacation on Friday and I'll be gone for two months," said Cooper.

"Cooper will show you around for now. I'll go and catch you later," said Bono as he left the shop.

Just then a small man came over to me and asked, "Are you the new instructor?"

"Get the hell away from us and get back to work!" commanded Warner as the man scuttled back to his worktable.

I noticed grins on the faces of Cooper, Warner, and also the guard, who had started to enter the shop at the sound of Warner's loud, angry voice. We left the shop and continued our tour. Outside in the hallway I asked Warner, "Why did you shout at the prisoner when all he did was ask me a civil question?"

Warner replied, "If you want to survive in this jungle, you have to show authority!"

This incident introduced me to the hostility that breathed on everyone in that prison. The tour was over at about noon; Warner suggested that I go to the officer's lunchroom and meet him in half an hour on the Cage Floor.

CHAPTER 4

THE KU KLUX KLAN

The Cage Floor is located at the front of the prison, about forty feet away from the main door. At this location a Watch Commander operates the security of the prison. Keys to all locks in the prison along with guns, radios, and gas bombs are kept in this special cubicle, within this designed cage. It is secured with locked doors and steel bars on the windows.

Entering the lunchroom, I saw employees setting at numerous tables scattered throughout a large area. Food was selected from a typed menu at a counter on the side of the room. The only visible food was in a glass case containing desserts, pies and puddings. A guard operated a cash register while an instructor and inmates stood behind the counter taking orders. Behind them food was in preparation. I later learned that the cafeteria was also a vocational training site within the prison.

The food looked appetizing. I made my selection from a list offered and was told to sit down. An inmate would bring me the food. I found an empty table. I noticed several men a table away eating and not talking; they were uninterested in one another and just eating the food.

Moments later a large man sat down opposite me. He did not speak and his manner discouraged me from attempting to talk to him. A black inmate soon brought my lunch to me. He offered a little smile then retreated. He seemed harmless enough, yet when he turned away the man sitting opposite of me suddenly exploded in anger saying, "I'm going to get that mother f*****!"

"What did he do?" I asked. In answer, the man got up and left the lunchroom.

Later, when I told Warner about the incident, he advised me to avoid that man if our paths should cross again. "He's been here for six years," Warner said, "and while we know he's been a member of the KKK we can't do anything about him." More to think about!

Leaving the Cage Floor I once again had to pass through the yard to reach the Center Gate. I could not help noticing the many fruit peelings and paper wrappings on the ground. There was garbage of all sorts; it was worse than any ghetto. It was a dirty mess. At the Center Gate I was relieved to see a guard looking out the window from his sanctuary and another guard posted in front of the booth. They were a welcome sight.

When I finally got back to the shop Cooper, my supervisor, asked whether walking through the yard bothered me. The expression on my face answered his question. I was tense from that short walk to the shop.

"You're on the payroll starting now," he continued. "So let's get you organized. The inmates will be back for the afternoon session." He began explaining rules and regulations to me and though I tried to concentrate on what he was saying my thoughts turned to a prayer that my mother had taught me: "The

Lord is my light and my salvation, whom shall I fear?" I was ready to meet the inmates coming into the shop for their afternoon instruction.

CHAPTER 5

THE ATTITUDE

Later in the day I stopped at a table to watch an inmate work on a pair of shoes. I attempted to tell him the correct way of doing the procedure. Midway through my explanation, the man interrupted me saying, "Okay wise guy, show me!"

The shop was suddenly very quiet. Here was my first test, a showdown with an inmate and I knew that I had to keep my cool. This was the sort of situation Warner had told me about.

"Show your authority," he said. I didn't want any trouble with anyone. My response to the man was, "I'll show you how and deal with your attitude later!" I proceeded to do so and looking up, I noticed Cooper standing in the doorway of his office motioning me to come inside.

I finished what I was doing and went into the office. In what I thought was an unnecessarily loud voice, Cooper said, "Don't let that inmate bully you. Let me show you how to make out a misbehavior report."

A guard came into the office and interrupted us, so Cooper stopped talking to me. He left the office and in the next moment all the machinery was shut off. I was confused. It happened without any explanation. The security guard then called out, "On the tools!" Apparently this meant all tools must now be turned in. The command also involved sweeping and cleaning the areas and benches, followed by all the inmates forming a line to leave the room for chow.

The phone rang indicating that it was time to send the inmates to chow. The prisoners filed out of the room and I joined Cooper in his office. He was clearing his desk and made no attempt to resume our former conversation concerning the misbehavior report. I thought some sort of apology from me was necessary for attempting to correct the inmate, but as I started to do so Cooper abruptly left the room. The security officer, who had observed the situation, came in and was the first person to offer me any kindness that day by saying my name.

"John, we all have to work together. Cooper has been here for twenty-three years and is just a harness maker. I think he resents your experience as a shoe craftsman and was ticked off when you showed your experience trying to help that inmate. You were telling him how to do things that Cooper couldn't."

At least now I understood Cooper's attitude and was determined to watch my step from now on. When Cooper returned to the office he appeared to have quieted down and suggested we call it a day. I watched him lock up the shop and accompanied him to the Cage Floor, where he turned in the keys.

He said, "Take it easy, I'll see you tomorrow morning."

As I left and walked down the long hill to where my car was parked I thought of how confusing things were in there. I turned to look back at the prison on top of the hill and asked myself, "What the hell am I doing in here!" I wondered how I would feel about returning in the morning. Could I really handle this job? By the time I arrived home I realized I had to make a living for my wife and three kids and accepted the fact that I would return to the prison. I could only hope tomorrow would be better.

CHAPTER 6

THE DEVIL'S DEN

The early morning sun found me returning to the prison. The men arrived for the morning class and Cooper turned them over to me. My confidence grew as the day progressed and things seemed to be going smoothly. The guard sat at the front of the shop and I noticed that whenever the telephone rang inmates looked up from their work expectantly. Later I understood why. Similar to being summoned to the principal's office when we were kids at school, inmates were ordered before the disciplinary board to answer charges of committed violence. The telephone also signaled visitors, a hospital call, a guidance counselor's messages, or the arrival of a package.

When a guard entered the shop an inmate said, "There's that a**hole who wrote me up!" I could hear what was said, but the loud noise from the machines covered the voice, protecting the ears of the guard from the outburst.

During the week Lt. Warner stopped by to ask how things were going. He suggested I contact him if I needed any help when Cooper left at the end of the week.

"You'll find your own teaching methods," he advised. "Let me know how they work."

At that moment two inmates started arguing. The guard pulled his nightstick as he jumped up from his post, saying,

"Knock it off you two or you'll find yourself in Keep-Lock." The men stood there a moment with clinched fists and then backed off, returning to work. The rest of the inmates were very quiet and work resumed. I could feel the tension in the room.

"Why don't you lock them up?" I asked.

"If it had gotten out of control I would have used my radio and called Center Gate for help to back me up," the guard said.

The week went by fast and my confidence grew as I found myself more in command of what was expected of me. Cooper seemed satisfied and stayed in his office during the day. Friday rolled around and Cooper left for his vacation. I would be alone to start the week.

Monday arrived. I reported for work. I drew my keys from the Cage Floor and once again walked through the yard to the shop. I was in charge I thought.

When the class arrived that morning I told them to sit down. They looked at me strangely. Some smiled. I took a roll call while they were sitting down, which seemed strange to them because they usually stood at attention at this time and answered "here" when their name was called.

I continued. "The shop has to keep a weekly production quota in making shoes for the institution. My job is to teach you how to make shoes and I thought you might be interested in learning about the history of leather and shoemaking. Also, how would you men like to make leather projects for your families? If

I could get permission for administration, would you be interested?"

I had their interest. And just when I started to explain the possibility about jobs in this field, the shop door opened and my supervisor ordered me to come to his office later. When the morning session ended I approached Bono in his office and before I could close the door behind me he blurted, "What the hell do you think you're doing?" He continued, not allowing me to speak. "You have a quota to meet by the end of the week. You better have it by Friday!"

I tried to explain that I was two weeks ahead of my quota for making shoes, but Bono dismissed me with a wave of his hand so I returned to my shop. The only reason I could think of as to why he was mad at me was because when he came into my shop the inmates were sitting down when they should have been standing. I brought my own lunch that day and ate it in the shop's office.

After lunch the second shift arrived for the noon session. Once the shop was in progress I entered my office and did some paper work. Now and then I looked up and peered out the office window to check on the class. The guard was present and the afternoon went smoothly.

My supervisor and administration were not interested in what I had to offer to inmates in making leather products and gifts for their families or teaching them a trade for vocational employment when they left the prison. They gave me no reasons why it could not be done.

For the rest of the summer it was touch and go with my supervisor and inmates. Each morning I would give a short talk following roll call about how prisoners could have more productive lives when they were released.

Near the end of the summer rumors were going around concerning new reform bills, rules and regulations for staff and prisoners. The inmates would have more control of the prison. Administration would be given additional paper work. Supervisors would monitor disciplinary reports and ensure that the rights of inmates were not violated. My supervisor and other department heads had their paperwork doubled; additional information was required on new forms for the records kept on all inmates.

I got through that summer with few disciplinary problems and report writing. My impression of inmates that first summer was that while babysitting, watch your back and keep them busy.

CHAPTER 7

THE EYE OF THE STORM

For the rest of the year I continued working at the factory on the day shift and my shoe shop four nights a week.

Friends and relatives frequently asked me about the prison: "What is it like working in a prison? Does it frighten you?" Working in a prison is like working in a small town isolated from civilization. The prison system is practically self-reliant and inmates have almost no contact with the outside world. Chills go up my spine every time the steel doors shut and lock behind me as I pass through. However, unlike the prisoners, I am able to return to civilization everyday after the shop closes.

As time went on, and it was getting close to the summer, I wondered whether I would be called back to work at the prison again. The summer of 1967 arrived and I received a call from Mr. Paul Doan at the Elmira Reformatory, asking, "Do you want to work the summer?" I agreed to try it again. I kept my job at the factory and continued working at my shoe shop while renewing my job at the prison.

On my first day back at the prison I reported to my shop in the morning. The same guard, Joe Gray, who worked with me last summer, began to tell me that Cooper did not like my method of teaching. And when inmates asked whether I was coming back he seemed reluctant to acknowledge my return.

As inmates began to report for work I greeted them and, while taking roll call, noticed many were missing from last summer. I asked about them and was told that one was paroled, three were in a serious fight and were in a special housing unit and the rest were transferred to other prisons.

I told the class, "We have three jobs that must be done daily. I have a trade to teach you, we will make shoes and do shoe maintenance repairs." Just as I finished saying that several inmates from last year called out, "Don't forget the leather crafts." I told them that it would be up to administration to O.K. that program, but I would continue to ask for it.

Following my shoptalk everyone went to work. At noon the class left for chow. That afternoon the P.M. class reported for work and I repeated the same thing I told the morning group. They appeared interested in what I said and the afternoon went smoothly.

At most of the supervisor's meetings I listened to many different questions asked by trainers and answers given to my fellow workers. I felt confused about the teaching method I was to use. I decided to study what the prison system wanted. My other concern was the security system. How did it work?

At the end of one of their meetings, Bono, my supervisor, told me to come to his office early the following day before the turnout. His boss would be there also. I reported to the office the next day and noticed a few instructors sitting around in chairs discussing procedures in the prison. I wondered whether I could bring up the subject of leather craft again, but decided not to do so at that time.

At the end of the meeting, as I was leaving, Doan asked me about the leather craft program. As I explained my plans, my boss interrupted us: "The inmates are turning out. You better get to your shop." That was a signal for me to keep quiet. Doan, however, patted me on my arm and said, "We will talk about this later."

Walking back to my office I was puzzled over Bono's reactions to the leather craft program. I could not understand my supervisor's reluctance to talk about the program. Could it be that he had to follow orders omitting the program? Was it a lack of funding or did he just want to show his authority? I knew the program would not cost much and it could be incorporated with the craft of making shoes and repairing them. All I could hope for was that one day, when a new leather program was started, the craft would be included.

For the rest of the summer I kept a low profile, waiting patiently for Doan to talk to me about the new program. By the last week of the summer there was still no word from Doan. I did not want to go over my supervisor's head and talk to his boss about the program. Doan had said he would talk to me about it later.

During the last week at my job I took inventory and was way ahead on my shoemaking quota for the summer. This would help Cooper when he returned for the fall program. On the last day of the summer I completed an extended quota. The inmates finished cleaning the shop, all tools were accounted for, my paperwork was up to date, and I had about an hour left before mid-day chow. I decided this was a good time to give a lesson in leather craft to the class.

I told them to be seated. Earlier I had cut out a pattern for a saddlebag from old pieces of leather. "As I promised you, I have been talking to administration about leather craft, but have very little information from Doan." I explained that the shop would remain under shoemaking until administration said differently. Since we had some extra time I would teach them a little about leather crafts. As I demonstrated the various steps and machines the men appeared to be interested and started asking questions. I felt good. When they left for chow that morning all they talked about were leather crafts. The afternoon class went smoothly and also showed interest in my demonstration.

At the close of the day I completed my security check, locked up the shop and preceded to my boss's office to turn in reports. Bono, my supervisor, and Doan, who was also there, both said, "You're doing an excellent job, John." I left their office and proceeded through the yard to the cage floor. When I reached the middle of the yard, some inmates held one arm in the air with a clinched fist and shouted, "My man, Pecchio." I let them know I heard them by acknowledging the gesture intended to show approval.

As each metal gate closed behind me I felt disappointment at being unable to complete the leather program I wanted to share with the inmates.

While waiting in line to punch out on my timecard other employees said they looked forward to seeing me again next summer. I started my walk down the hill to my car, thinking about what I had learned that summer.

I realized that if I was to continue a career in the prison system I needed to understand how prisons operate under stressful conditions, including life-threatening situations. This was hard to accomplish because I only worked about eight weeks in the summers. Inmates at that time seemed more content, making a less dangerous atmosphere. I began to empathize with some inmates, making me understand their needs and what they expected of me as an instructor. At the end of the summer I was getting good results in expanding my curriculum to keep things running smoothly in my shop.

CHAPTER 8

INTO THE FRAY

One summer while on vacation in Canada with my family we visited a museum. Even on vacation I was reminded of my job in the prison. Employees wearing garments that identified them with wartime eras acted as guides. Following one of the guides we entered a dungeon located down a long flight of stone steps. There we saw confining chains and iron restraints used on prisoners held in small cubicles. A storage room filled with odd weapons was included in the tour. Spears, knives and shields were among those shown. What was notable was an assortment of smaller items similar to those still made by inmates in the Elmira prison. Of particular interest to me was the cloth-braided rope. Several of them contained curved steel rods at one end that were used for scaling walls during an escape.

There were numerous steel rods sharpened on one end. Thin, flat stones with edges grounded to a cutting edge, tied to handles made from pieces of wood reminded me of confiscated weapons I had seen in our local prison. Escape and protection are on all prisoners' minds. These weapons are still made by prisoners today.

On the way home from our vacation I purchased a newspaper and noted an article which reminded me of the problems with the judicial system in regards to prisoners.

According to the report, an inmate had a stomachache and asked for pain medication from the hospital. Following an examination by the doctor he was treated with a liquid to correct the problem. The prisoner objected to the liquid, obviously seeking drug assistance. The inmate is now suing the medical staff at the prison for being treated unfairly. This lawsuit should have been settled in the prison, not in an outside court.

On June 19, just before the summer programs started at the prison, I got a call from Mr. Bono asking whether I would work again for the third summer in a row. He also said Cooper was resigning later in the season and wondered about my interest as his replacement full time. The job offer excited me. I accepted and started that following Monday. In Mr. Bono's office that morning he told me that Mr. Doan had retired and Mr. Bradley was the new Director of Education.

Going home at the end of the day some instructors and teachers were walking through the yard talking about Mr. Doan's retirement. They noted that Mr. Bono was not pleased that Mr. Bradley got the position. This caused a lot of tension between Bono and Bradley for a long time. For a few years I had many dealings with Mr. Bradley and thought he was okay. But as time went on he became a pain in the butt.

Bono knew how to play both ends against the middle and he did just that with Mr. Bradley. Every time a problem came up with an instructor he shifted it to Bradley, knowing he was only trained in education and not in the vocational area. If Bradley made the wrong decision he would look bad in front of his boss, Mr. Coleman, who was in charge of all programs in the prison. Bono would have a smile from ear to ear when this happened and act as though he had nothing to do with the problem.

Bradley needed help in the vocational area and Coleman had to depend on Bono for assistance. Bradley had only five or six years in the prison system while Bono had about twenty years of experience.

I continued to work that summer and stayed out of their way. The last day of the summer, Cooper called the prison and told Bono he would finish out the month of October and retire. My boss asked me if I wanted the job full time. I immediately said yes. I started full time on October 2, 1969. Now I could give my two weeks notice to the factory where I worked and then transfer extra work to my shop at home.

The news pleased my wife. She and the children said they looked forward to having me home more often. The prison offers a good salary and the state pays for my college courses to teach in the vocational field. In addition, the state provides medical insurance and paid holidays. Life was looking good. If only I had the sense to realize what I was getting into.

On my first day back at the prison full time, I was standing on the Cage Floor with other employees waiting for the guard to unlock the gate; we were told there was trouble in the yard. We would have to wait until it was cleared up.

Moments later, a prisoner with a bloody nose, who was

held in an arm lock by a guard, was shouting, "When I get loose, I'll get you're a** for this!" A second guard appeared for backup and the men moved past our group. The sight was one of many that I would witness in the future.

Arriving at my office, I explained the situation to Bono, but he had already heard what happened and knew that a lock down was due for that day. I tried to enter the shop to join Cooper, but the door was locked. When he opened it to let me in, he explained, "When things like this happen, we have to lock all doors."

About an hour later inmates began coming in and Cooper suggested that I take the roll call and get the opportunity to look them over. I noted that many were the same inmates who had been in the class the year before, but there were several new faces among them.

Later that morning Cooper asked me to give a shoptalk to the prisoners during the afternoon session instead of taking out the tools. He had been informed that "inmates turn out" was due at some time that day and it would be easier to exit the room without worrying about the security of shop tools. He also asked me to use the time to give the men a talk about making shoes. The idea appealed to me, but also put me on the spot. I did not want to make Cooper uncomfortable by challenging his teaching style and appear to know more than he did about leather.

I began my talk about shoemaking and realized that the men were becoming bored. Realizing that my talk was going nowhere, I changed the subject to leather and how it plays a part in our everyday lives.

"Shoemaking comes under the subject of clothing. You'll always have a job making shoes and be able to provide for your family. Everybody needs shoes. Learning how to use the machines that make shoes will give you an opportunity to branch out into all types of leather products as well. Leather has played an important part in all the wars fought in our country and in others. Army tanks use at least 90% leather for their interior construction. Battleships require large amounts of leather. Leather straps for seats, gun holsters, jackets and fly suits require leather. It's an insulator as well."

The men began to ask questions about leather and making shoes. It was a good exchange. At one point I told them that a black man was responsible for inventing the shoe. He discovered that leather felt good on his feet and took more abuse than pieces of cloth. Later, the comparison between rubber and leather was made when the trade recognized that rubber boots and shoes caused the feet to sweat and leather allowed feet to breathe.

An inmate asked, "How do basketball players keep healthy feet, wearing sneakers with rubber soles?"

I told him, "Only the soles are rubber, the rest of the sport shoe is made of canvas cloth and leather uppers that breathe. The top part of the shoe is called a vamp and the sides are called quarters." This extra bit of information appeared to sit well with the class. Cooper was pointing to his watch, indicating that it

40

was time for me to stop.

The turn out period had begun and as the men left the room I thanked them for participating in my talk. In exchange I received some very strange looks. Later, Cooper told me that inmates have never been thanked before.

As I left the shop that day Joe Gray, the guard, said, "Join me for lunch when Cooper leaves. I've been here for seventeen years and I'd like to share some advice with you about the inmates." Cooper left at the end of October, which would culminate in his retirement. The following Monday morning I reported for work, drew my keys for the shop and started my walk through the yard. Things seemed to have quieted down in the prison. The morale of the employees and inmates seemed to have improved following the lock in.

Officer Gray was off for a few days and on Friday of that week he was back to work. When the inmates left for their midday chow he said he had brought his lunch with him and asked if he could eat it in the office with me or did I prefer to go down to the cafeteria. I replied that he was welcome to join me in the shop.

I also brought my lunch to work that day.

At lunchtime Gray did most of the talking and I listened. He used to think inmates were like animals in a cage and some are, he said, but "you learn to separate the good ones from the bad. If you show you are interested in them, you'll be amazed at how well they'll respond."

He continued, "Pressure behind bars can make an inmate dangerous to a point where he becomes a manipulator, a jail-wise prison lawyer. A survey made by the Central Office revealed that not only did inmates appeal their cases, but were actually suing the administration for institutional harassment. The criminal justice system was involved and had to check into the prisoner's records for evaluation."

As time passed Gray continued to share his lunch periods and the information he passed on was very informative. For instance, he stated that some inmates were serious thinkers concerning their families. These inmates often paid a privileged prisoner, who had access to the law library, to help them secure information that might help get a reduced sentence. The name "Fish" was given to a new inmate who was doing his first bid. It was a normal procedure for scams or swindles to be used on the new inmate to frighten him into paying for protection through more experienced prisoners. The frightened newcomer, wanting to survive, would too often give into the demands made upon him.

Deranged inmates were the dangerous ones and hard to handle. Often an inmate would request protective custody, but was denied because he could not prove harassment. He was told that he had not been in long enough and to just "give it time."

A prisoner's counselor comes by about once a month to check with his assignments and advise inmates, "If you go into protective custody, you have no privileges, schooling or vocational shops. You are confined to the block and a cell twenty-four hours a day. When you have to see a doctor or need to travel around the facility you have to be escorted by a guard." Basically, prisoners are told to keep quiet and serve their time.

It is not uncommon for an inmate to take his own life rather than submit to the persecution suffered from older and experienced prisoners who choose the victim for their special brand of entertainment.

Attempting to defend himself, the victim might have to see his Review Board for an assessment of his institutional records. The number of misbehavior reports he has accumulated due to his attempts to defend himself is considered. I absorbed all of this from Gray as he continued his monologues as time went by.

It was a point of interest to me that the prisoner was never given the opportunity to defend any of his actions or explain why they had happened. The board apparently folded their arms, turned the man down for any action taken in his favor and he was told to be ready for another report in the next six months. Usually he was marked as a complainer and transferred out to another prison where his indoctrination would begin all over again.

One interesting case occurred shortly after I had taken over the class following Cooper's retirement. An inmate, Jerry Morre, had been transferred to Elmira from another prison. He had been assigned a guidance counselor, but seemed to know the ropes and no one was bothering him. He showed up in the shoe shop a couple of weeks after his arrival.

When an inmate arrives in prison and puts in a grievance against another he is in real trouble. He is labeled a "snitch" and word gets around fast. It does not matter that he is right about his complaint, but he is a marked man. When Morre entered the shop that morning he had a black eye and blood on his face. He asked to wash up at the sink and I gave him permission to do so, asking, "What happened?"

He replied quickly, "At school yesterday I was standing at the door in the classroom and bent over to pick up a book when the door opened. The knob hit me smack in the eye."

I replied that his black eye looked as though it had just happened. I let it go and sent him to work. When the rest of the inmates arrived and were busy working I used the shop phone to call the cell block officer where Morre locks and asked, "Was there any trouble in the block this morning?"

"There was an inmate stabbed," he replied.

I mentioned Morre had a black eye. The officer said, "We think he did the stabbing." Other officers will be right over to pick him up.

Within a few minutes two officers came and took Morre to Keep-Lock. He was silent as he was taken away. The following day Morre went to a disciplinary hearing.

The Lieutenant explained the charges against him and asked, "Did you stab the inmate?"

"It's a set up."

The inmate said you stabbed him and four other inmates said they saw you do it.

"Tell the truth and we can help you," the Lieutenant said. Moments later, Morre broke down and confessed to the stabbing. His story was that the prisoner had been harassing him for months, wanting cigarettes and sexual favors. He had tried to get his cell changed, but was repeatedly refused by his counselor who advised him that there was a limit to the number of times he could change his cell.

He told how he had to stay away from this inmate who kept on pushing him, irritating him until that morning.

"He had come up from behind," Morre said, "shoved me back in my cell, held a steel shank to my neck saying, "suck my d*** or you're dead."

"That did it," continued Morre. "I got hold of the shank he was holding. We wrestled to the ground and I stabbed him in the stomach three times. Then I hurried up to the shop."

As the story goes, the inmate stabbed by Morre did not die, but he was crippled for the rest of his life. Morre got twenty years to life added to the five years he was serving for robbery.

A year or so later Morre was found hanging in the armory. Prison officials called it suicide. Early complaints should not be labeled. All complaints should be treated seriously. The professional unfounded complainer will soon be found out. Morre paid a high price for defending himself. Why should misbehavior be hidden by the system until it erupts? Without hope or support all behavior changes.

Inmates go through a lot of stress from the day they enter prison and leave. Out of all that leave prison 95% return for a second, third and fourth bid.

According to the Central Office's reform committee before an inmate is released from prison he must have a place to stay either at a parent's home or a close relative. Following parole the inmate is required to report to the parole officer at stated periods. He is given a set of rules to follow, which includes the strict omission of drugs and alcohol.

In some cases families do not want that individual in their midst, so they lie about their presence to collect welfare as a family member. Turned loose, the former prisoner wanders back to his old associates and ways that got him into trouble and ends up returning to prison.

CHAPTER 9

FULL TIME AND PERMANENT

In October I became a full time employee under the title of Vocational Instructor in Shoemaking at the prison. The work schedules were the same as public schools. The work period involved ten months, with two months off for summer vacation without pay. I would still receive pay for the holidays and could accumulate up to one hundred and fifty days for sick time.

For the first five years I took off for the summers and the shoemaking shop was closed down. Then I started working year around. The school calendar gave me enough time off to suit my needs.

During the fall program my boss came to give me a performance evaluation. He told me that Cooper had died the previous night of a heart attack. I commented on how sad that was since he just retired. Half an hour later the evaluation was done and he left for the day.

When working for the State of New York prison system it was mandatory that all new employees serve a one-year probation period. If a bad evaluation or reprimand for any wrongdoing was received the employee was permanently dismissed. I was lucky and finished my probation time in six months, due to Bono's good evaluation of me.

After becoming permanent the Vocational Instructor is

47

required to take college courses for a teaching certificate. I needed thirty-two credit hours and another thirty for a trade test. I started the college courses within three weeks: going two nights a week for three years, attending Boces College programs in Elmira, monitored by Oswego College in New York State. This never interfered with working days at the prison. Before I finished the college courses I was supposed to have taken a trade test in shoemaking and no one in the State was qualified to give me that test.

Central Office then called me to visit them. When I got there I was asked to write an outline in shoemaking. I did so and upon completion of the course outlines, along with my ten years experience, and Superintendent Mattison's high recommendation of me, I completed all the requirements needed to become qualified for the job. My title was "Vocational Instructor in Shoemaking." Two weeks later I received a letter of congratulation from the superintendent.

When you become permanent the only way you can get fired from the Department of Corrections is by committing a crime, or by being charged with a serious disciplinary action brought on by the department heads or inmates. In some cases, if the disciplinary action charges are not too serious, the Inspector General Offices and Management will give the employee options — pay a fine or receive a written warning. If you accept their terms you keep your job. As time passed, all the prisons were changing; the system was being updated. The name

"Reformatory" was changed to "Correctional Facility." The prison where I worked was now called "Elmira Correctional Facility and Reception Center." A guard was now called a Correctional Officer. Uniforms were changed from dark blue to an all-gray color, with one black stripe down the outside of the trousers.

Inmates could attend work release programs and work outside the prison at different jobs and return to prison at the end of each shift. New prisons and "Shock Incarceration" camps were being built along with the remodeling of the old prisons. When an inmate was qualified he was transferred from a maximum or minimum prison to one of these camps. After he satisfactorily completed the program he was paroled.

College programs for inmates were in full gear. Even though most taxpayers could not afford to send their own kids to college they still had to support a prisoner's college education, as well as pay for their incarceration. This did not make sense to me.

Most of the prisons in the State were changing their policies in the medical field. We were right in the middle, standing next to inmates with diseases that were not detected at this time. Other inmates, who were already identified with diseases, were being treated for tuberculosis (TB) and AIDS that was becoming prevalent. We were not trained to handle the mentally disturbed.

I remember, at the time, how the prison leaders tried to

downplay the TB syndrome telling Correctional Officers, and all employees, "If you have contact with an infected prisoner, get a TB shot."

It was hell when employees working in classrooms or shops were told by administration to keep a tight security watch on infected or mentally disturbed inmates. In the past, the instructor had been notified ahead of time when an inmate who was mentally unstable was assigned to a program. This was discontinued.

Misbehavior reports were the only means to control the behavior of inmates throughout the prison. An employee could no longer use any physical resistance to protect himself. One of one of the new changes stated that if you are attacked by an inmate and badly hurt, and the inmate stops and just stands over you, you are not allowed to assist in any punishment upon that inmate. If you do you are fired.

CHAPTER 10

NEW SYSTEM – NEW PROBLEMS

The Disciplinary System was being changed again. This time it was called "Tier System 1-2-3" — the higher the number, the more serious the crime. We were given an inmate rule book and told that with every misbehavior report written we must choose a rule and put the number next to it and explain in detail what happened. The Keep-Lock system was introduced. This meant that prisoners were locked in their cells and very few were locked in the Guardhouse.

In Tier 1 misbehavior reports you could not lock the inmate in his cell, but had to turn in a report, hoping the inmates got called in a week or so, before he made any more trouble in your classroom. In that time period a block Sergeant would see him and he would get a warning or be kicked up to the next step.

The sad part of a Tier 1 is that the inmate still had the same attitude. If he went for a hearing with the block Sergeant and returned in an hour or so he would tell inmates, "The employees have no juice." (That meant no control, power or connections.)

In Tier 2 the inmate was locked up and a report was sent in that day. Then, within seven days, he was called to the disciplinary board, which sometimes deprived him of commissary privileges and recreation. If he was not called after seven days he was released.

Tier 3 was a superintendent's hearing. The inmate was locked up indefinitely and a report was written. The superintendent or another high-ranking officer then summons him. If the superintendent could not make a decision the final step was that the inmate was tried in an outside court and sentenced with more time, or the charges dropped.

The most common statements made by an inmate after being written up were: "I was set up," "He (or she) is prejudiced," "I didn't feel good at the time of the report," and "My rights were violated!" The board was under pressure due to all the written reports on inmates and it did not want them writing to the Central Office. In most cases the brass would downplay reports on the inmate and a lesser sentence would be given.

Before this, when a misbehavior report was written on a small pad, it involved putting just the inmate's name, number, block, cells, with the number of the rule or rules he violated and a signature. The guard took the charges as he escorted the inmate to the "Guardhouse," where the offender was locked in a cell for about thirty days. After that he was ready to work and did not want more trouble. The program ran smoothly and we had fewer disciplinary problems.

Central Office knew that the tier system was not going as expected. The reports and frivolous lawsuits were backlogged up to three years or so with no relief in sight. So they came up with a program that would help the employees: all employees had to attend classes in stress training 1-2-3 IPC (Inter Personal Communication), chemical training, self-defense, harassment, report writing and first aid. With all the courses taken by employees for jobs in the prison system not one was ever given on how to handle or prevent inmates' frivolous lawsuits. Why were state lawyers representing prison employees who were only doing their jobs?

Another nightmare was the State Legal Aid system, which defended the prisoner's legacy by going along with their fantasies, lying to the courts to protect their rights. It was a farce when an inmate swore on a Bible to "Tell the truth and nothing else but the truth, so help me God."

I believe that with better planning 99% of the frivolous lawsuits filed by inmates should be and could be handled by the Correctional Facility's Disciplinary Board or by the Superintendent at the prison instead of the courts. There is no end to Central Office's prison adventures. They seem to enjoy playing both ends against the middle. First, they threaten prison officials who are doing their jobs and come down hard on employees who do not follow their orders. Then they try another scare tactic by stating that prisons throughout the State will be laying off employees, followed by a new case scenario.

Employees were pressured to work out of title, which included feeding inmates in their cells during lockdowns, searching cells with correctional officers, and sweeping inmate blocks. On top of that our recreation time was taken away. We were ordered to do more work and search for contraband in other parts of the prison. Inmates went to recreation only once a week for half a day. The time was used to prepare job lessons, check shops for contraband and conduct repairs needed on machinery, etc. Employees involved in out of title work put in grievances with their Unions. Central Office, politicians and labor management were involved, and after a lengthy session the employees won the battle, but were still losing the war.

Central Office was not happy with that decision. After a few months they came up with another plan. All shops were going to do maintenance work along with keeping our regular programs going. This new program was called "on the job training for inmates." We already had maintenance workers at our facility trained for such jobs and had prisoners working with them. Central Office was well known for using scare tactics on department heads and employees, especially when they wanted to win a decision.

Security had been going downhill because guards were doing extra duty and could not cover their assigned posts. The prison needed more correctional officers. Now, with programs about to be shut down, inmates would be left idle to parade around the facility in large groups. A Security disaster could happen at any moment.

Central Office devised a method to assure that no further repercussions would come from the new maintenance programs and guards complaining about security. The first thing they did was to put an article in the newspaper stating, "State does not have enough money in the budget and will cut back on programs and security employees in the prisons system."

The unions had second thoughts about going along with the complaints from an employee after reading and talking to Central Office about layoffs. Now they were telling employees to stop complaining about security and maintenance work and worry more about the layoffs.

Despite the entire extra duty and work the employees were doing our pay grade remained the same. The prisoners started complaining to Central Office about the extra maintenance work and asked to be paid more money for their involvement. Without any complaints from Central Office they got a new pay scale throughout the facility.

No layoffs occurred and a few guards were hired, but regardless of that civilians had to do maintenance work. We became servants of the prisoners and of the administration.

For the past eight years I accomplished many goals. I wrote a Shoemaking course outline in English and Spanish. All types of dress shoes, sandals and leather projects were on display in my shop and were exhibited at fairs around New York State. More than once the superintendent visited my shop with Bono and Bradley. I remember two visits before the summer vacation of 1978 when Central Office's inspection team came to tour our prison and were very impressed at how much progress had been accomplished in the shoemaking shop.

Bono and Bradley took all the credit for the program, saying how much hard work they put into setting up the shop, and never mentioned my participation. I was silent and just shook my head thinking how many times I had asked for help from them and been turned down.

I made up a card system for inmates to sign when they entered and left the shop. On the back of the card was a list of tools, leather projects, and materials. When ordered they could study the charts. It was useful in teaching the trade. When inmates told department heads that I was not teaching them the cards proved otherwise.

On several occasions, when Bono and Bradley visited my shop, they would ask, "Where do I punch in?" and laugh. I joked back because this was the way I kept my cool.

One day an inmate wrote to Central Office complaining that he wanted out of my shop, stating I was not teaching him anything. I sent the card system to Central Office and the inmate was locked up for lying. The superintendent praised me for the card system.

When Bono and Bradley received notice from the superintendent that an inmate complained I was not teaching him he mentioned how well he liked the card system. From that day on, when my boss or Bradley visited my shop, nothing more was said about it.

Chapter 11

CHAOS

Mr. Jack Coleman, the Deputy Superintendent, was going to retire soon and wanted to stay until his replacement, Brad Johnson, learned the ropes. Johnson was a tall man, well over six feet, spoke with a deep voice and was a man of few words. He said what he wanted and you followed. He already had more than ten years of experience with the prison system and understood the new changes along with the problems we were facing.

Bradley was doing his usual up front motivation to Central Office and Department heads when he wrote an article in the prison newspaper that was read by all concerned and pushed other prison leaders and employees to use humanistic, compassionate and rehabilitating methods.

At the time he wrote those inspiring words I had hurt my back at work and continued to work while wearing a back brace. In the middle of winter we had a snowstorm and a lot of people could not make it into work. I reported fifteen minutes late and Bradley climbed all over me.

Apparently those humanistic and compassionate methods he had written about were not going to be imposed on employees working with him.

One day I had permission from Bono to leave the facility

fifteen minutes early to go to the Credit Union Office for some personal business. As I walked to the credit union I noticed Bradley sitting in a chair at Nine-Post, a small building located outside where a guard greets visitors and watches all who go in or out of the facility. I kept on walking to the credit union next door when Bradley opened the door and began shouting and shaking his fist at me in front of guards and visitors. "I will see you in my office at eight A.M. tomorrow morning," he yelled at me.

I hurried over to him saying, "I had permission to go to the Credit Union from Mr. Bono because they close the same time our shift ends." I suggested he should call him, which he did, but he was not finished with me. I continued to walk over to the credit union. When I got there the clerk hurriedly helped me fill out an application and asked for my driver's license number. I said, "It's in my car, I'll go get it."

I started down the hill where my car was and once again Bradley poked his head out the door, shouting, "It's not four o'clock yet. Why are you leaving so early? I'll see you in my office at eight A.M., tomorrow!" and slammed the door shut.

I poked my head in the door and said, "Stop threatening me like a kid!" and turned away. I continued walking to my car and drove it up to the credit union to find it had closed. I went back to Nine-Post, and into the facility looking for Bradley, who had apparently left for the day. The guard at the door asked me why I was still at the facility at 4:25 and I tiredly told him, it is a long story, "I'll tell you about it some day."

The next morning I attended a meeting with Bono and Bradley at the office. When I got there Bono was sitting in a chair and Bradley wasted no time in having his say. He began shouting and pounding his desk saying, "You know that your hours are from eight A.M. to four P.M."

I tried to explain that I had permission from Mr. Bono. I looked at Bono, waiting for a confirmation from him. He just sat there and said nothing. Bradley hurriedly said, "We already talked about this. I am going to put a counseling letter in your file."

"I'll write a rebuttal and file a grievance with the Union if you do," I replied.

"You have been warned about this type of action before. Go on to your shop. Inmates are running." The meeting ended.

As I walked to my shop many things went through my mind. Why was Bono not speaking on my behalf? Why was Bradley yelling at me?

During the ten years I had been working with the department I never had a single counseling session, or any performance evaluation stating I was abusing my time. And now, having created the best shoemaking shop in the State, they both had a personal vendetta against me.

The next day I received the counseling letter and carbon copies were sent to the superintendent and deputy superintendent for programs. Without hesitation my supervisor had put my counseling letter in my personal folder at the personnel office. I called the Union and discussed the matter with Robinson, the union leader, who said, "Write your rebuttal, give me a copy, and later, if needed, we can file a union grievance."

This is a copy of the counseling letter, from Mr. Bradley, word for word:

Date: December 5, 1979
To: Mr. John Pecchio, Instructor IV
From: Mr. Bradley Educational
         Director
Subject: Counseling Session

This is to record and confirm the counseling session, which was held in the Central Education office, Wednesday Morning, December 5, 1979. You and Mr. Bono, Educational Supervisor (Vocational), and I were in attendance at this session.

At this time you were counseled pertaining to your failure to comply with rules and regulations governing early dismissal. We specifically referred to your performance on the afternoon of Tuesday, December 4, 1979. Mr. Bono acknowledged giving you permission for early release on Tuesday afternoon to visit the Credit Union Office and your presence at the office has been verified. However, you spent only a few minutes in the Credit Union and exited the Facility at 3:48 P.M. via crossing the front lawn to the parking lot. As you were leaving the Facility I called to you to ask that you report to my office tomorrow morning. Shortly thereafter you drove to and parked your car in front of the Facility. Before you re-entered the Facility you came over to nine-post, opened the door and said, "Stop threatening me like a kid," and then slammed the door.

You were reminded of similar violation when, only a week before, on Tuesday, November 27, 1979 you left the Facility, without permission, at 3:45 P.M. On Wednesday Morning, November 28, 1979 in this same office, Mr. Bono and I informally counseled you on this event. You acknowledged that you had previously been informed and were aware of the 4:00 P.M. dismissal time rule.

A copy of this counseling session letter is being placed in your personal folder with additional copies being sent to Mr. Warren, Superintendent, Mr. Johnson Deputy Superintendent for Programs Services, Mr. Bonus and Educational Supervisor (Vocational) Personnel Office.

I wrote my rebuttals and sent copies to the same, asking Mr. Warren if he would please take the counseling letter out of my personal file or I would have no choice, but to put in a Union grievance. These are some of the topics I covered on this misleading counseling letter:

Why did Mr. Bradley, pounding and shouting at me in the office, seem so determined to give me a counseling letter for leaving the facility early even after he'd acknowledged that Mr. Bono gave me permission?

Why did Mr. Bradley not take into consideration the statement that Mr. Warren had made during a staff meeting? "We are all professionals, and don't have to punch in or out on time clocks, but must put in a good 8-hours worth of work!"

If I arrived at the facility every morning at 7:30 A.M., a half-hour before my schedule time, why was Mr. Bradley so worried about me leaving twelve minutes early?

Mr. Bradley mentioned how he and Mr. Bono have counseled me in the past about leaving the facility early. Why was it not written in my performance evaluation and a counseling letter put in my personal folder at personnel like this one is?

Mr. Bradley said, "I left the facility at 3:48 P.M." We talked twice for a few minutes, once leaving the facility to go to the credit union and another time going down to the parking lot to get my driver's license.

The distance from the front door of the prison to the credit union is about one hundred yards. From that point I walked two hundred yards to my car and it took another two hundred yards driving back to find the credit union closed. I had to walk another one hundred yards back to where I entered the facility.

He does not mention why I entered the facility looking for him and he was nowhere in sight. I then started to walk out of the facility and the officer at the door asked why I was working so late since it was 4:25. I said, "It's a long story, I will tell you sometime." How could I have done all this in twelve minutes?

Mr. Bradley does not mention why he was sitting in Nine-Post, in a nice warm building looking out at the scenery, while his professional staff was working and needed his assistance.

Here is the Superintendent's response to my letter.

> This is in reply to your letter to me on December 6, 1979 concerning a counseling session and letter.
>
> I have asked Deputy Superintendent Johnson to investigate this matter on my behalf and he has advised me that he did discuss this with you and took appropriate action to resolve it to your satisfaction.
>
> I hope you will keep in mind the seriousness of the position you hold in our facility and perform your duty in a professional fashion at all times.

The counseling letter was removed, but no copies were sent to the union and I was never notified from Personnel office that it was out of my records. This matter was overlooked and not mentioned by Bono and Bradley.

The very next day Bono and Bradley came to my shop, telling me to send inmates to recreation. They wanted to search my shop. I asked, "What for? Thirty cans of Tuna-fish and sticks of pepperoni?"

"I've got to investigate an inmate's complaint against you," said Bradley.

I continued getting my tools in and a few feet away Bradley was talking to inmates Rainbow and Jones. Other inmates were standing all around listening and wondering what was happening. I overheard Bradley asking Rainbow and Jones,

"Did Mr. Pecchio sell you those belts you're wearing and did he charge you for them?"

Both replied, "Yes."

I finished checking the tools and inmates left the shop for recreation. I went right over to Bradley and began shouting at him, "How could you be so inconsiderate, asking inmates right in front of me and the whole class listening, if I sold them belts? And why didn't you consult me first instead of treating me like a criminal?" He just turned away and, with Bono, walked into my back storeroom searching.

Then it dawned on me: tuna fish and pepperoni are what inmates pay other inmates for contraband.

I proceeded to the back room and Bono, who has been in this room many times before, wasted no time asking me, "What is that refrigerator doing in a shoe shop?"

I replied, "It's been here for years. You know that I still keep the glue in it so it won't dry out and because it is highly inflammable. I do occasionally keep my lunch bag in it."

He said nothing and opened the refrigerator and started pulling all the glue off the racks, putting them on the floor. He even looked in my lunch bag and found nothing but two sandwiches and an apple. Handing me the bag he said in a stern voice, "Get rid of the refrigerator now."

I tried talking to him, asking, "Why now; you could have told me that a few years ago." He looked at Bradley as if he wanted him to say something, but Bradley said nothing. "Okay, you're the boss. I'll have it out by the end of the day."

Bradley and Bono continued searching. I said, "Can I help you look for the tuna-fish and pepperoni?" I started pulling stacks of leather from the top shelves, throwing them to the floor. Just then they stopped searching and went to the outer office, finding nothing.

I followed them into the office. Bradley said, "Close up the shop and come with us, we're going to get to the bottom of this."

"Where am I going and get to the bottom of what?" I said.

"To Mr. Johnson's office," he replied.

As we proceeded to Johnson's office I kept repeating, "This is a set-up and you know it. I'm completely innocent and I never sold any leather project to any inmate."

"We'll see," he replied.

When I got to Johnson's office I noticed that Mr. Robinson, my Union Steward, was sitting in a chair. I said hello to him and sat down.

Mr. Johnson asked me, "Do you know inmate Jones?" and gave his number to me.

"Yes, he is one of the inmates that worked in my shop. I locked him up for stealing leather," I replied.

Then he asked, "Did you threaten and ask Jones to give you the phone numbers of girls in New York City?"

"No, Sir! I thought this meeting was about selling leather to inmates for tuna fish and pepperoni. How did these girls get into it?"

He looked at me strangely and said, "What pepperoni and tuna-fish? The only thing I want to know about is the girls' phone numbers. Jones had a meeting with Bono and Bradley and they handed me the report. It's their job to investigate all inmates' complaints on instructors and teachers."

I told him the story about Bono and Bradley's visit to my shop that morning and when I finished Johnson looked at Bono and Bradley with an angry expression on his face. He stopped me and said, "That's enough; I will be getting in touch with you after I make a decision. Go back to your shop and recall your inmates."

As I shook hands with Robinson and Johnson I remarked, "I'm sorry you were misinformed." Leaving the office, I shut the door and could hear Johnson yelling at Bono and Bradley. It made me feel good!

When I walked into my shop the phone was ringing. It was Robinson, the union representative.

"Bono and Bradley got a real chewing out. Sit tight and wait to see if charges are filed."

"Why can't we do something when Bono and Bradley are out to get me?"

"It looks that way, but we have to play by the rules. I am sorry, John; let's take it one step at a time."

I called the inmates back from recreation and noticed Jones was not with them. I asked the correctional officer where he was and was told that Jones had been called up by the Brass and taken to Keep-Lock for an investigation.

I motioned to Rainbow that I wanted to see him and asked the guard to watch over the other inmates while I talked to Rainbow in my office.

"Why," I asked him, "did you lie to Mr. Bradley, telling him I sold you the belts?"

Rainbow replied, "I wanted to get back at you for locking me up and writing a misbehavior report on me last week for stealing leather."

I explained to him how serious a charge this was and advised him to write a statement that he lied or a hearing would be held and the truth would come out. He said nothing. Chow was called and I sent him out with the rest of the inmates.

That night I had difficulty sleeping since I was thinking about Bono and Bradley who were constantly trying to set me up. I wondered why Johnson was not stopping them. If I did not get a handle on this I could get fired.

That next day I reported for work and, while taking roll call that morning, noticed Rainbow was missing. I asked the guard to check on him then got the class started and went over to the officer's bench where he informed me that Rainbow had been locked up for investigation.

Back in my office I noticed an inmate asking the officer if he could talk to me. I waved him in. He said, "I work next door and was asked to drop a letter off from Rainbow for you."

I thanked him and he left. The letter was a carbon copy of the one sent to Bradley. It said, in so many words, that Rainbow wanted Mr. Bradley to forgive him for making a false statement about me. And when Bradley asked him about the belts and food he was emotionally upset with me at the time and wanted to get back at me for locking him up. He wants to withdraw his statement, hoping the charges would be dropped against me.

I immediately made copies of the letter and sent them to Warren, Johnson, Bono and my union representative, Robinson.

That afternoon Robinson called and told me he had received my letter and could not see where I was in any trouble, but acknowledged that it did make Bono and Bradley look bad. He suggested I remain patient and he would keep me informed. We left it at that.

A week or so later, on a Monday morning at 8:00, I got a call from Bono saying, "You will not be having inmates today. Go to the Superintendent's Office for a meeting with the Inspector General. Mr. Robinson will be calling," and hung up. As soon as I put the phone down I received a call from Robinson, telling me to meet him on the cage floor at 9:00 that morning, and together we would see the Inspector General.

When I got to the waiting room Robinson and I talked for a few minutes and then went into the meeting. As we entered the Inspector General told us to be seated and began by asking if I knew the girls in the photos. "Did you call them?"

"No sir," I said.

He jumped up from the chair and, pointing his finger at me and shouted, "I can tell if you are lying or not. I have been in the business for fifteen years and I can judge if an inmate is lying or not."

That scared the hell out of me!

The Inspector General continued shouting at me, asking all sorts of questions, I had no recollection of what most of them were about. He finished and just sat in his chair writing in a note pad.

About ten minutes went by and he then repeated the question again, ***"DID YOU CALL THESE GIRLS?*** I can get your phone records from the phone company and check your calls in and out."

I again repeated, "No sir, I am being *set up.* "

He continued as though he never heard me and started on another subject. "Did you ever charge inmates for leather products and accept food from them?"

Again, I said, "No, sir."

"Do you have anything to say?" he asked.

"Yes I do," I replied. "I know nothing about the girls you're talking about, and do know that Mr. Bradley and Bono have interviewed the two inmates we're talking about, and here is a letter from inmate Rainbow telling Mr. Bradley he lied about me."

There was a deep silence in the room as he read the letter. He then put it into his briefcase.

"I'm going to take your picture to New York City and talk to these girls and see if you had any contact with them."

I replied, "Okay."

I was waiting in my shop for the Inspector General to call. It was about 2:00 when a call came from Mr. Robinson. He said, "I just received a phone call from the Inspector General, who showed your picture to the girls in New York City. Their responses were that they had never seen you before, or talked to you on the phone. Inmate Jones was lying. He told me to tell Pecchio that he is okay and it was all a set up."

Boy! What a relief. I wanted to file a Union Grievance against Bono and Bradley for abuse of power and harassment, but Robinson talked me out of it.

"John, you are going to be here a long time. Let it lay and chalk it up to experience."

I was furious, but knew the politics in prisons were so twisted that I had no choice but do as he said.

About a week later a correctional officer was escorting Jones to the tailor shop to be fitted for some clothing. He was going to an outside court for another charge.

When the officer was finished at the tailor shop Jones asked him, "Can I see the shoe man?"

"Okay," said the officer.

I was in my shop talking to Mr. Robinson at the time and saw Jones coming. I waved him in and he put an envelope on my desk, saying, "Sorry, Mr. Pecchio," and left.

70

Robinson and I opened the letter, which said, "I apologize for what I've done and hope that you will not press charges against me. This trouble started when Mr. Bono and Mr. Bradley questioned me on whether Mr. Pecchio had tried to get phone numbers and house addresses of some girls in New York City. I saw a way to get back at you, Mr. Pecchio, for Keep-Locking me."

All three major charges Bono and Bradley were pursuing were dropped.

CHAPTER 12

INTRIGUE AND DECEPTIONS

Within two weeks after the case with the Inspector General Bradley and Bono were setting me up again.

I was in my office talking to Sergeant Blue. I had just sent inmate Frank Lomain, a homosexual, on a pass to the hospital. Within minutes Lomain, came running back into the shop shouting that an inmate was trying to rape him in the hallway. I said, "Put this in writing and I will give it to the Sergeant. This is a security matter."

Just as I finished saying that, Stool, a correctional officer came running in asking, "Who threw the broken glass all over in the hallway outside your door?"

The Sergeant and I looked at each other and then turned back to the officer and said, "We don't know."

After Lomain had finished his statement and handed it to the Sergeant he was escorted to Keep-Lock by the Sergeant and the officer for safety reasons and would be released after an investigation.

My time card was due that day. Inmate Frank James, who I had locked up several times, was having trouble with another inmate in the class. To separate them I sent James to my boss's office with the time card sealed in an envelope. Apparently James had complained to my boss several times before about me locking him up. I did not know they both were scheming to get me. I found this out later.

Within ten minutes the phone rang. It was Bono. He began shouting at me, "Why are you not running your program?"

I replied, "I called in my tools because there was a problem and it was a security matter. The Sergeant was here and handled it and I gave a shop talk for the rest of the morning."

James should have been back by now. I called Bono and asked, "What time did James leave your office?"

"I had to lock him up for an investigation; he will not be back," he replied.

"What investigation?" I asked.

"You'll be informed when I get to the bottom of this," he said and hung up.

I continued my talk session until the inmates left for the afternoon chow.

I closed up my shop and on my way to the boss's office Bradley and Captain Jones met me at my door asking, "What is the matter, John?"

"If you mean about the inmate being attacked," I replied. "I have the report right here. I was on my way to Bono's office to get it signed by him and Sergeant Blue, who handled the security end."

Bradley put his arm around me and said, "John, we've been working together a long time now. I'll take that report." I handed the report to him.

I locked the door and all three of us proceeded to the front of the prison. Not one word was spoken on the way there.

When I got to the cage floor Bradley said, "They want to see you in the Superintendent's office."

"Who does and what for?" I asked.

"They just want to talk to you," he replied.

I went into the office where Johnson, Captain Jones and Robinson were sitting around the table. Bradley and I sat down and the meeting began.

Johnson said, "We are going to put you on sick leave for a few days starting now."

"What for?" I shouted.

Johnson replied, "Bradley and Bono thought you were acting very strange lately and I too thought you needed a rest."

I looked at Bradley and said, "This has already been prearranged by you and Bono. You both have been trying to get me for a long time ever since I made a fool out of you and your counseling letter to the Superintendent and the Inspector General. This is your way of getting back at me, isn't it?"

"John, I don't know what you are talking about."

There was silence in the room. Everyone stood up and left. The meeting had ended. Johnson and Robinson escorted me to the front door and told the guard in the cage room that I was going on sick time and would be locked out.

As I started out the door Robinson said, "I will see you tomorrow. The head man of the Union, Mr. Green, will be here

74

at eight o'clock in the morning and he will escort you into the facility."

The next morning Green and I went right into Superintendent Warren's office. Green asked, "What charges do you have on Mr. Pecchio?"

He replied, "No charges; we only put him on sick time."

"Then why is his name on the door as a lockout and not permitted to enter the facility?" Green asked.

"Tomorrow I'll give you some answers," replied Warren.

We left and talked outside for a few minutes. Green said, "Take it easy, you're getting paid for this, I will be in touch. Go home and rest."

"You sound like the department heads, telling me to rest, but from what? And why was I being locked out without a charge?" I said.

"I'll call you tomorrow," he replied.

Green did call me the next morning at home and told me that he was talking to his boss, James Taka, who agreed with him.

"You're on vacation with pay for the Christmas holidays. Don't return until January 2, 1980."

"That is fifteen days from now. If the Superintendent puts me on three days sick time then why was I on lockout for the other twelve days of a vacation time without a charge? You know that your name is not supposed to be on the door and lockout of the facility if you're on sick or vacation time."

75

Green replied, "They have not given us a reason why. All we can do is file a union grievance."

That was it. I had many sleepless nights until I returned.

On January 2, when I went back to work, my name was still on the door as a lockout. I had to see Johnson before I could be allowed into the facility.

"How do you feel?" he asked.

"The same way as the day you locked me out," I replied.

"You were not locked out, but put on sick time for three days. Go back to work."

"I don't understand; how come you and the Superintendent keep telling me I was on three days sick time? When I returned for work this morning my name was still on the door as a lockout and I had to be escorted into the facility to see you."

"When you're on sick or vacation time your name should not be on the door as a lockout. If you're on sick time for more than three days you must have a doctor's slip before returning to work."

"How can you put me on sick time? You're not a doctor of medicine, just in education. Doesn't that bother you?"

"You have not seen a doctor? Wait a minute." He went into another office to use the phone. A half hour later he returned. "You'll have a physical in the Central Office in Albany, New York, on January 14, 1980. Go back to work and keep a low profile."

"That physical is ten days away; if I am still sick how can you put me back to work without a doctor's orders?"

He was really angry by now and shouted, "Go back to work and keep a low profile. You won't have inmates this morning, not until the afternoon session."

I could see he was not going to admit that he was wrong and was more concerned about covering up his mistakes. Sending me to Central Office for a physical was one way out for him.

I went back to work and called Robinson, my union steward. We talked about the set up by Bono and Bradley. In the last part of our conversation I stated, "Nobody has asked me or seems to want to hear my side of the story, or from two witnesses, Sergeant Blue, and officer Stool, who were in my shop at the time of the problem."

He replied, "You will have your say at a grievance hearing soon, and will get your sick time back. Take it easy, you're in the driver's seat."

About ten minutes later Bono called and said, "How are you feeling?"

I answered, "The same way as the day I was locked out on sick time."

"You will have inmates this afternoon," he replied.

The 14th of January arrived and there was no word from the union or administration. I went for my physical and the medical doctor asked, "What's wrong?"

I told him the story. He said, "Well, at least you will get a good physical out of this."

At the end of the examination he made a statement, "You are as strong as a bull. Go back to work and I will send my report to the facility."

"I'm supposed to see a psychiatrist; how do I get there?"

"See the nurse in the hallway."

After receiving directions I took a taxicab to the psychiatrist's office located across town. When I got there a nurse greeted me and when I explained who I was and why I had come she told me that the doctor had committed suicide.

I asked to use the phone to call the Elmira Correctional Facility. I explained that the psychiatrist I had been sent to see in Albany was no longer available. He had committed suicide. I asked to be directed to another.

"Go back to the hospital and someone will direct you to another psychiatrist," she replied.

Returning to the hospital I was directed to another psychiatrist and again took a cab to his location a short distance away.

This time I was lucky. The doctor was in. After waiting almost an hour before I could see him he reviewed the information about my case received from the Elmira Facility.

"Who is this Mr. Johnson in this report?" he asked.

"I was sent here because a mistake was made and I was locked out of the facility and put on sick time without a charge," I explained.

Shaking his head he said, "They do this all the time when they screw up. What happened?"

I told him, "You are the first one who would let me tell the story and ask if I had witnesses."

When I finished he said, "Why didn't you tell them this story in the first place?"

"I tried to but was cut off every time I asked if they wanted to hear my side. Apparently they were more concerned about setting me up and locking me out," I replied.

Shaking his head he said, "Go back to work; I'll send my report to the superintendent. You're okay."

I took another taxicab back to the hospital and then to a motel. All I could think of, besides how upset I was, were the taxpayers having to pay for all these expenses: flying to and from Central Office, meals, lodging, cab fairs, the Inspector General's investigation, secretaries and most of all, the time wasted with department heads involved in concocting this set up.

I returned to work, still without a doctor's slip, and immediately filed a union grievance to get my three days sick time back.

Two weeks later, after several meetings, Johnson, Robinson and Deputy Superintendent of Personnel, Fred Jessey, called me again for the last and final meeting. They told me they had the medical report back from Central Office Medical Staff. I was not sick. My sick time was reinstated on the books. End of meeting. Superintendent Warner, Bradley, Bono, and Johnson only got a slap on the wrist and left me alone for a while.

To finalize the union grievance the Union lawyers and Central Office could not tell me what charges I had for the lockout. I could not sue or file another grievance on department heads because I never lost a nickel or any sick time.

The incident was still on my personal file without a charge for years after it all happened.

For a long period of time my lockout by the department heads was the talk of the facility and, of course, the inmates found out and made their remarks.

When walking down the blocks and passing cells I could hear them say, "There goes the bug," meaning I had to see a psychiatrist. I could never catch them because the inmates would wait until I got a few cells away from them before they said it.

Walking further I noticed a couple of signs high on the walls with cartoon pictures of a man on a horse carrying a stick of pepperoni and written on the bottom of the sign were these words, "Pecchio the pepperoni kid rides again."

When I got to the end of the block where the guard was standing I asked him if he could have the inmates remove the pictures. He said, "I certainly will."

I wrote to Commissioner Thomas E. Gold in Central Office Department of Correction, telling him my story, and was told, "It is being handled at the facility level and by the union."

Talk about politics! *CASE CLOSED*.

CHAPTER 13

A BREATH OF CLEAN AIR

In February 1980, Deputy Superintendent Coleman was retiring. Coleman's father, Jack Coleman Senior, was the Superintendent at this prison and had retired years ago while his son was still working.

I never met Coleman Sr., but the stories I heard about him were so impressive that I could see why he was honorably respected by so many. Here is a story I will always remember.

One day Coleman Sr. received a call from Central Office telling him they had received a letter from an inmate complaining about a guard using brutality on him. He replied, "You worry about Central Office and let me worry about my prison," and hung up.

He went right down to the Guardhouse where the inmate was located. Coleman Sr. stood outside his cell, calling to the officer standing at the end of the block controlling the electric levers to all cells, "Crack his cell." (To crack a cell means to open it.) He walked up to the inmate and slapped him in the face, telling him, "If you ever write one of my guards up again you will answer to me!" From that day on the inmate never bothered any employee again.

The current administration leaders heavily depend on Central Office to make decisions for them. They are in constant fear of losing their jobs if they make a wrong decision when disciplining inmates.

For instance, one day the superintendent was faced with a problem that involved him. He was walking down the block in the Guardhouse and as he passed under an inmate's cell bodily fluids were tossed out of the cell at him. He went home to shower and returned to call Central Office asking for help. They said, "Put hard tempered plastic in front of the cells and that will solve the problem." He did just that. Later, because of the hot weather and no air getting through the bars, inmates' grievances and accusations of inhumane treatment were brought into it. The plastic was removed from the Guardhouse's cells. But the situation was still the same and at any given moment body fluids and feces; could come flying from the cells.

I wonder what Coleman Sr. would have done. Now Coleman Sr.'s son was retiring and, like his father, is admired by many. On Coleman's last day of service he was asked by the press to make a statement about his thirty years experience working in the prison system.

> He said, the way it is now, the more intelligent inmates harass the less intelligent and create problems for employees. A correctional officer can walk into the middle of a disturbance and not know whether the troublemakers are intelligent, mentally defective, or borderline. The changes over the years have resulted in problems with low morale and discipline. The decisions handed down by the courts have weakened the efficiency of the control over inmates. It's damn difficult to run a facility or try to help an inmate. We need additional

industrial shops and staff to keep prisoners busy. Too many inmates don't want to do anything and they don't have to. An adequate staff would save a lot of money in the long run compared to what it would cost the State if one of these joints blew up in a riot. The biggest problem with employees today they know what should be done, but it's tough to do it." Coleman continued his response to reporters, "At one time we had damn good morale. People were proud they worked on the "Hill" (Hill was another way of describing the prison), but that's not true today." Inmates today, he said, "are more emotionally unstable."

Coleman continued talking about the new prison reforms for inmates. Summarizing his thirty years of service he said, "I feel I did the job I was paid to do and helped those who wanted to be helped."

That was a good speech and described the prison system exactly as it was and remains today.

After reading Coleman's statements it reminded me of the day he talked to all the vocational instructors at a meeting. He told us to "follow the guidelines of Central Office's Philosophy of Vocational Education." He had written a guideline for distribution that stated,

> Our goals in Vocational Training are to provide training, retraining, and upgrading opportunities to secure employment in society for inmates. An accurate report must be kept on how many projects, tasks, and levels the inmate has completed. All records should be kept on unusual incidences in the Vocational Shops, e.g., punctuality, dependability, getting along with others, working as a team, being neat and clean and maintaining good health. What is also

significant is giving an honest day's work, showing loyalty to the organization, knowing how to use materials and equipment, working under pressure, adjusting to work situations, managing time and materials, following safety regulations. All together, the education of an inmate must aim to improve his self-esteem.

Well written. As the days and months passed all the vocational shops were well into the maintenance program. When another instructor needed something from my shop to help him complete a project I was willing to help. When a project was completed and delivered, depending on how heavy it was, one or two inmates delivered it unescorted. Security and my boss never interfered.

CHAPTER 14

HELL CONTINUED . . .

One day the Art Class instructor, Paul Branch, was in my shop admiring a leather nameplate on my desk. We were on good speaking terms then so he asked me to make him one to put on his desk. The nameplate was a strip of leather about two inches wide, ten inches long, and a ¼ inch thick. Branch had made many signs for my shop when needed and Bono always approved them.

On my lunch hour I took a piece of scrap leather from a garbage bag, stamped his name on it, let it dry and glued it to a piece of scrap wood. I would tell Branch that night after work that his nameplate was done.

I had a hobby shop in my home and Branch and Bono knew this. At the time clock I told Branch the nameplate was finished.

"Could you cut me five plain leather belts for my wife to engrave for Christmas presents? Tomorrow morning I will leave my back car window open in the parking lot so you can put them through," Branch said.

The next morning before I entered the facility I put the leather in his car and proceeded into the facility to my shop. After all the inmates arrived and were working inmate Frank Stroud came over to me. "Could I take the stamped leather plate to Mr. Branch; I have some papers to give him," asked Stroud. I was very reluctant, knowing how I Keep-Locked him several times in the past. What was he up to now?

I called Branch and told him I had put the belts in his car and he could pay me at the time clock that evening.

He asked, "How much do I owe you?"

"Fifteen dollars," I replied.

"Okay," he answered.

"I will send inmate Stroud over with your name plate. He also has some papers for you," I replied.

Later when Stroud returned I looked at his pass and Branch and Bono signéd it.

I asked him, "Why were you in Bono's office?"

"He called me into his office as I was passing by and he asked questions about you," he replied.

"What questions?" I asked.

He said, "They were nothing; just asked how I was doing in the shop and were you giving me any trouble."

Stroud then handed me an unsealed envelope with $15 in it. He told me, "This is from Branch for the belts."

I was very disturbed so I told Stroud to go back to work. I then called Branch immediately.

"Why did you send the money for the belts with an inmate? I was going to meet you at the time clock tonight. I don't like inmates knowing my personal business and handling money for me. I could have lost the fifteen dollars," I stated.

"My clerk saw me put the money in the envelope and give it to Stroud. It should all be there," he replied.

I told Branch, "Bono was talking to Stroud on his way back from your shop and he must have noticed the money in the envelope. I hope nothing comes from this," I said.

Branch said, "I've got to go, I have a problem with an inmate," and hung up. I could tell he was nervous about something as we talked.

At this time I did not know that inmate Stroud, Bono, Bradley and Branch were plotting against me.

Nothing happened for the rest of the day. I closed up shop and left hoping I could talk to Branch at the time clock.

When I got there he was nowhere in sight. I asked several employees if they had seen Branch.

One said, "I saw him in Bono's office as I walked by."

I left for the day and the next morning Bono called me at 8:00 sharp saying, "Stroud will not be coming to your shop this morning; he was locked up last night for an investigation."

I asked, "What investigation?"

"I had a long talk with Stroud last night and he was upset with you. I thought it was best to lock him up," he replied.

"What did I do to upset him? He was fine when he left for chow yesterday morning."

"He was very upset when you sent him to pick up the fifteen dollars at Branch's office for the belts and you accused him of stealing ten dollars," he said.

"That is not true; I sent Stroud to Branch's office to give him the nameplate I made for his desk."

"That's a lie! I already talked to Branch and he said you called telling him you lost ten dollars."

I called Branch and told him that according to Bono I had accused Stroud of stealing the $10 he sent me for the belts.

"Why did you lie to Bono about the fifteen dollars you sent me?"

"I thought I heard you say you lost ten dollars," he said.

I replied, "I told you, I could have lost all the money and I don't like inmates to know my personal business."

"I misunderstood you; I will call Bono and explain."

For about two weeks every time I saw Branch and Bono they were always in a hurry and could not talk to me. It was obvious they were trying to avoid any conversation with me.

When I brought my inmate's payroll and paper work to Bono's office on Friday I got the same silent treatment.

Two weeks later after the incident I got a letter from the Inspector General's Office and Bureau of Labor Relations in Central Office. The letter stated that I was being fined in the amount of $200 for the following charges:

> In accordance with the Disciplinary Procedure, Article 33 of the agreement between the State and PEF, Union for Professional, Scientific and Technical Service Unit, (This is the same title for Vocational Instructors) you are hereby informed that we will implement the following penalty:

1. You directed Inmate Stroud to go from the leather shop at the Elmira Correctional Facility to where Mr. Branch was the instructor for the purpose of receiving from Mr. Branch fifteen dollars in cash for delivery to you. In so doing, you demonstrated poor judgment in that you caused the inmate to violate institution rules prohibiting inmates from having money in their possession. Further, you abused your authority by sending an inmate to perform a personal chore for you.

2. Subsequent to receiving the envelope from Inmate Stroud you accused him of having removed ten dollars. During the succeeding days you attempted to pressure the inmate to return the ten dollars or to replace it with items of comparable value from the commissary.

3. When questioned by your supervisor (Bono) concerning this matter you made a false statement, specifically, you denied having accused the inmate of removing ten dollars from the envelope.

4. When you engaged in the above-described activities you acted contrary to the following section of the Employees' Manuel: 102.6, 201.11, and 202.5

5. If you wish to dispute the proposed penalty you may file a disciplinary grievance according to the provisions of the disciplinary procedure, which is article 33 of the unit agreement. Such a grievance must be filed with me and postmarked no later than fourteen calendar days from the receipt of this notice at the close of the appeal period.

At the end of this meeting I had many thoughts. I could

not afford to lose my job and I knew that I had done nothing wrong. It was a set up again. Why was I being punished? Branch sent the $15 with an inmate; I had never asked him to do that! Now I was being accused of pressuring the inmate.

I had my suspicions about who was doing this. It had to be Johnson. He was the only one who would call Central Office about this meeting. He got his information from Bono and Bradley. Branch was brought into it by Johnson indirectly telling him to play along if he wanted to be promoted.

I fought back by filing my grievance with the Union within the fourteen days allowed.

A week later a union representative from the main office, Kate Cover, came to the facility to interview me and attend a meeting with the Inspector General of Labor Relations.

We went over all the charges and the best she could say was, "One hundred people go through the stop sign and you are the 101st and you got caught."

About forty-five minutes later Cover came out and told me the charges would be reduced to having an inmate do a personal favor for me. It would cost me $150 instead of $200. With reduced charges I could keep my job.

"What punishment did Branch receive?" I asked.

"Under the circumstances he got off with just a verbal warning," she stated.

If ever there was a case of power abuse by prison leaders playing politics with mandating rules and regulations, this one was flat out ridiculous.

I understood that I would have $15 taken from my paycheck for the next ten pay periods. The union was in agreement that filing a grievance would only add fuel to the fire.

CHAPTER 15

THE PRISON LANDMINES

Superintendent Warren was retiring. His replacement was Gregory Mattison from Central Office. Mattison was a determined individual who would stop at nothing to enforce Central Office's rules and regulations. Many employees at the facility thought he was giving the inmates too much control.

One of the programs he started was an inmates' Liaison Committee. The inmates would choose a leader to represent their complaints. These leaders were issued special cards signed by the superintendent giving them special privileges to travel throughout the facility to investigate problems. The superintendent would meet once a month or sooner with the group and try to resolve the issues before they got out of hand.

At first it seemed like a good idea. As time went on and inmates were receiving all kinds of favors from the superintendent they began calling him "The Candy Man."

Within a short time the program was starting to become a security risk. Central Office and their chain of command were concerned about the increasing demands of inmates and asked why the misbehavior reports were becoming backlogged.

The superintendent was now faced with major problems. He was conducting too many hearings on inmates' complaints and could not solve them fast enough. Inmates were becoming too smart for their own good; they walked the prison like they were untouchable. Long periods of sitting in their cells waiting for administration to render decisions made them very nervous. The superintendent had no choice but to shift a large portion of the inmates' complaints to his security staff. Liaison leaders were taking advantage of the issued card signed by the superintendent, running throughout the facility without escorts, listening, dealing, and pressuring administration leaders with their demands. The Liaison leader would walk into a classroom unannounced with inmates standing all around and show his card to an instructor or teacher asking to rectify an inmate's complaint. It was even more stressful when he did this on employee lunch hours without security present. This, for sure, was a real security risk.

If the Liaison leaders were not too impressed with the employee's answers he would schedule a meeting with the superintendent or another high-ranking prison official and express his views. If necessary, the superintendent would then schedule a meeting with the employee in hopes of resolving the inmate's complaint.

I could never understand why Central Office and the superintendent wanted a liaison committee. The prison always had its own disciplinary board to handle all inmate problems. Central Office dreamed up this program and now had to live with it or take it away. But how could they do this without causing a riot? Once you give or promises a prisoner something, then decide to take it away, they look at it as a punishment and will stop at nothing to get it back. So Central Office came up with a way to slow the Liaison committee down in hopes it would eventually be terminated.

First, the inmate leaders had their card taken away. Then, all meetings had to be requested by the inmate leaders and scheduled by administration at their convenience.

For ten years the unorthodox methods I had to endure from prison leaders and inmates had been very stressful. I certainly did not take this job to challenge and solve administration blunders. I was thinking about a career.

When I took this job my determination and dignity were far more important to me than just walking away. I continued working on a professional level and tried to keep a low profile, but the very high risk in challenging inmates and administration's leaders was a losing battle.

The chances for surviving in a prison always depend on common sense. Training must be taken very seriously or you can develop a sense of paranoia. Life threatening situations in most cases will have some sort of a warning signal. The secret is to know how to quickly recognize and deal with warning signals, such as inmates becoming very restless, wanting to be locked up and trying to distract you so other inmates can work their plans.

Prisons, like most large businesses, have become a paper world. Constant decision-making required daily records and documents to justify every movement in the facility. It was phenomenal. The day I checked my personal file with Mr.

94

Robinson and the Labor Relations man left me dazzled. The horrendous amount of documentation and misleading information placed in my folder along with how the labor relation man was throwing it out and making his derogatory remarks toward administration leaders made me see just how the prison leaders operated.

I asked my union representative, "Why didn't I get copies of all this information that was in my folder? Isn't that the way the rules are supposes to be?"

Robinson just shrugged and said, "Yes, but nine out of ten people are scared to death of arguing with them."

I then asked, "Why is it, when I revamped my shoemaking shop into one of the best shops in New York State, and when I was asked by Central Office in Albany to write my course outline in shoemaking, and I did it in English and Spanish, it was well accepted with not even a note in my folder? But if I lose a wallet, or a tool and have the tool returned, several prison leaders write all sorts of documentation and practically trip over themselves to get to the personnel office to enter their letter into my personal folder."

Some people suck up to their superiors to get special favors and recognition to further their careers. If that is their goal in life then that is their problem. I never had to or wanted to; I was too busy doing my job.

A supervisor's personal remarks greatly influence an employee's reputation and experience through the evaluation reports, which end up in the personal files. If his remarks are unfair or biased and you do not know about them they remain as an uncorrected part of the record. That fact is really hard to beat. It is part of your career until you are retired or fired.

Considering the number of times experienced and intelligent prison leaders take advantage of their employees always amazes me. We all work in the same prison. We count on each other for survival; yet why do some supervisors become so deceptive, manipulative, thrive on power, spend state money, and play politics? Central Office has its own set of rules. They will never admit to any mistakes and know how to manipulate situations to their advantage and disrupt any differing thought.

When an employee is brought up on charges or called to testify against another employee personal records are brought into it. The bosses produce records along with their recommendations. But when a scheduled meeting is called where the employee can explain his version of the problem the employee is only allowed ten to fifteen minutes to tell his side of the story. The constant interruption by the Inspector General concerning rules and regulations contained in the prison system is mind-boggling. Actually he seems to be irritating the employee in an attempt to make him lose his temper rather than seeking an impartial judgment.

One day the Federal Government sent all prisons in New York State a notice that extra money was available to keep inmates out of their cells for longer time periods. A committee for the programs was formed at our prison and Bradley was in charge. He had to report to the superintendent periodically to make sure the money was well spent. Within two weeks night programs were underway.

A leather shop was one of the programs. An instructor was hired. About ten days into the program Bradley asked me if I would be interested in taking over the night leather program, which was to run four nights a week for three hours each night.

I replied, "Sure, when do I start and where is the inventory list?"

"You can start tomorrow night. The teacher left in a hurry and never turned in any reports or a tool inventory. I couldn't find it anywhere. Let's just say that's water over the dam. Make up a new list of tools and materials you'll need and have them on my desk tomorrow morning." Then he handed me a shoebox of tools and materials.

"These are all the tools I have to teach with?"

"Let it be; as I said, its water over the dam," replied Bradley.

The next morning I took the list of tools and materials needed and placed them on Bradley's desk.

I asked him, "What do I teach with in the meantime?"

"Use your experience; teach out of books until your order arrives. I will send this order in today."

I replied, "I will borrow some from my shop and replace them when my leather shop order comes in."

"That's good; I'll be talking to you."

After a week into the program I asked Bradley, "Did my order come in yet?"

"I sent it in and put a rush order on it. I can't understand why it's not in yet. I will check on it and get back to you."

I could not help but feel very suspicious about the way Bradley was handling the night programs. Too many other teachers were complaining about not receiving materials. He was hiring unqualified instructors that were untrained for prison work and handled dangerous tools and materials without inventorying them. That, for sure, was trouble and could become a life-threatening situation.

Where was the money going for the night programs? I knew Bradley's reputation. I dealt with him and Bono too many times and, after their set ups, I could not trust his opinion. He was more concerned about pleasing the Superintendent and Central Office and making sure his report looked good on paper in order to keep federal money flowing into the state prison system.

My clerk, Tim Morke, was my tool man. When an inmate is picked for a tool man in a shop a certain amount of trust is involved. So when he told me that our night class instructor was always leaving tools and materials laying around, making it easy to steal the items, I realized there was a serious problem.

I was very curious about how many tools were missing. I did not waste any more time. After the inmates left for chow that afternoon I went out front to the purchasing department and talked to the clerk, Jim Apples.

I asked, "Could you please find me the orders Bradley put in for my night program?"

He replied, "Sure, just a minute."

A few minutes later he returned with my regular folder for the shoe and leather shop and pulled out the night leather class inventory and said, "That order was canceled by Bradley."

"What is the night leather class doing in my Shoe and Leather program file?" I asked.

"That is the way Bradley wanted me to set it up," said Jim.

I began looking through the folder and read the night leather class inventory. I could see that about 90% of the tools were missing. I asked for a copy, thanked him and left.

That definitely put me on the alert. At first I was very angry with Bradley. Was this another cover-up for the missing tools? I went back to my shop and called Mattison, the superintendent, saying, "I would appreciate it, sir, if I could talk to you about a personal matter. Only you can help."

"Will tomorrow be okay? Call me in the morning when you get to your shop," answered Mattison.

The next morning I called as ordered and he said, "Come down during your lunch and preparation time, we will talk."

I was prepared when I got to Mattison's office. I had the copy of the tool inventory for the night's leather program, the shoebox I received from Bradley and a letter addressed to the superintendent telling how Bradley canceled the order when he had promised me he would send it in. Bradley and Bono's mailbox were next to the superintendent's office. I put copies of the letter into their boxes and went into the superintendent's office.

I gave him the letter and showed him the shoebox of tools and materials Bradley gave me asking, "How am I supposed to teach forty inmates with just that? I thought with ninety percent of the tools missing this was a very serious matter. When I talked to Mr. Bradley he just passed it off as water over the dam."

Mattison said nothing, picked up the phone and called for Bradley and Bono, shouting at them to come to his office immediately. I just sat there. A few minutes later he went out of the office and returned with Bono and Bradley.

Mattison said to Bradley, "Go next door to the purchasing department and find the tools and materials list you ordered for Mr. Pecchio's night leather program."

Bradley said, "Sure."

And as he started out the door, I said, "You won't find any orders. You canceled them."

The look on his face said it all. Mattison told Bradley to go next door and find the order and bring it to him.

He told me to go back to my shop saying he would call me later.

Bradley returned as I was leaving and Bono just sat there

100

in a chair silently. He would not look at me, but I could see by the expression on his face that he was really mad.

I left and as I shut the door I could hear Mattison yelling at the top of his voice at Bono and Bradley. I felt nervous wondering how they would try to set me up again!

I was in my shop when the phone rang about half an hour later. It was Bradley. He began shouting at me.

"What the hell are you doing telling the Superintendent about the night program's tools?"

Before I could answer him he hung up.

Just then Bono came walking into my shop also shouting at me, "What do you think you're doing, going to the Superintendent complaining about tools and materials. Haven't you learned anything yet about going through proper channels?"

"That's what I tried to do and nobody would listen," I replied.

"Because of you the Superintendent is shutting the facility down tomorrow morning and will have a tool search throughout the prison. Johnson is very angry with you."

"Why are you making me the bad guy here? You should be helping me. You know the danger involved if someone is hurt with a green-handled leather knife. Will you and Bradley back me up? I think not."

He walked out, shaking his head, slamming the door behind him.

Like clockwork Bradley called again, still shouting, "Give

me a list of tools and materials that you need. Have them in my office before you go home tonight. This is the wrong time card you gave me."

"It's the card Bono gave me," I replied.

"When you bring the list over tonight I will give you the right one," he said, slamming the phone down.

I called Mattison and told him, "I couldn't work under the pressure that Bradley and Bono were putting me through because I talked to you about missing tools. They are harassing and shouting at me every time I turn around."

"You did the right thing, John, be patient with them. They are under a lot of pressure right now. If you need me just call; I'll speak to them."

About fifteen minutes later inmates were reporting for roll call when Bradley called, again, and sounded very pleasant.

"Take your time in preparing the materials and tool list. You can have until tomorrow afternoon. I will send you the correct time card."

The next day I had plenty of time to make up a list for Bradley while the facility was being searched for weapons. That day I talked to Bono and he, too, talked in a normal voice.

The outcome of the search: about 90% of the missing leather tools were found and returned to me. I received a call from the superintendent thanking me for following through on the missing tools.

A week later I received my new tools and materials.

Three weeks later I received my order. The night program was canceled. I kept the leather tools and materials and used them in my regular program.

Knowing how the system works I realized it was a matter of time before Bono and Bradley would find a way to get even with me.

CHAPTER 16

POLITICS AND THE CENTRAL OFFICE

New York State budget talks began on January 1 and passed by April 1 of that year. Most of the time the budget is delayed and costs the state and taxpayers thousands of dollars in interest on borrowed money to keep the prison system going. This keeps the prison staff guessing and working in a very tense atmosphere.

Crime is on the rise in this country. Prisons are becoming overpopulated and constantly need more correctional officers for security. When Central Office refuses to hire more correctional officers everybody gets involved: unions, employees, media, administration and politicians. If the pressure is too much for Central Office to handle you will see fewer officers hired to calm the situation.

One year the budget was passed and no money was allocated for extra officers. Administration leaders had orders to cut back on eleven correctional officers' jobs and double up on security positions. In addition, no money was allowed for overtime, sick leave or vacation time. The security heads were furious. Correctional officers and unions filed grievances, but very little was done. This, for sure, placed the prison in a dangerous situation.

It always amazes me how the state budget department in Central Office sets its priorities at budget time. One year they cut back on officers and security to build a new gym for inmates, costing approximately $1.5 million, and thought this was money well spent. The reason given: to replace the old brick gym building because it had been condemned. Leaders of the prison viewed it differently. They were convinced that the real reason for the new gym was because it had been torn to shreds during a sit-in confrontation with inmates and cost too much to rebuild.

Prison staff, officers and the unions desperately complained to Central Office's that prison security was hurting and the fact that more guards were needed. Too many areas were unguarded causing potential life-threatening situations. For example, they mentioned that the Tailor shop and my Shoe shop had dangerous weapons, tools and knives. Each shop had always had a guard. With the budget cuts there was only one guard for both shops and now, months later, that same guard was covering five shops.

Superintendent Mattison was asked by security leaders, "who is going to cover all the inmates and keep up with security problems if the guard layoffs continue?"

His answer, "There is nothing I can do about security right now, I just have to deal with the prison cuts as best as I can do."

Let's look at some Security prison situations that should not be taken lightly at budget time by Central Office leaders.

In January 1986, for example, a prison in Moundsville, West Virginia had a riot and sixteen hostages were taken. Some of the hostages were released and seven hostages were left in prisoners' hands. The reason inmates released only part of the hostages was because the governor of the state promised to meet with them. The rioting lasted for two days. During those two days three inmates were killed before the hostages were released. They murdered other inmates. One inmate carved up a prisoner who was accused of being an informer. Another inmate was dragged up and down the cellblocks as other inmates kicked and spit on him before cutting his throat.

While a guard hostage was blindfolded he tilted his head back and could see the weapons (homemade knives, spears and clubs) made by inmates. The inmate, who was cutting out another man's heart said, "It's amazing how this little thing will keep a fellow alive." There was blood all over. Guards prayed that one of them would not be next.

This type of inmate exists in all prisons, Federal or State. Thousands of these violent prisoners will overpopulate the system as crime rates in the country increase.

The main function of sending a criminal to prison is to control his behavior. This is the first principle and necessity.

More correctional officers should be hired to deal with hardened criminals, instead of building a new gym for them, thus improving upon their physical strength but leaving them without disciplined supervision or work to contain their energy. They should be disciplined and worked as they once were.

It is inevitable that prison employees will file union grievances at one time or another against the system while trying to keep their dignity intact defending their rights in the agreed contract between the state and union. The reason for the continuing stress is because prison leaders know how to delay the grievances and extend them well beyond the time limit instead of promptly dealing with them and solving them. They use delay for control advantage. In the meantime the problems keep building up while some grievances are put on hold indefinitely.

Prison employees do realize the challenges of facing dangerous circumstances with inmates that may lead into a potential death trap. Quitting is not always the answer. There will always be more employees hired who will face the same dangers.

Suffering mental and physical stress while working in a prison is devastating and no human being should have to endure such pressure in life.

CHAPTER 17

THE PROBLEM GETS PERSONAL

One day in February 1983, I received a call from Mary Leasy, the superintendent's secretary. "John, a sheriff from the county wants to talk to you; can you come to the superintendent's office?"

"What did I do now?" I asked.

"When you come to the office I will tell you, okay?"

I arrived at the office and the Sheriff was standing there with a paper in his hand.

"Are you Mr. Pecchio?"

"Yes sir, I am," I replied.

"I have a summons to serve you pertaining to inmate Tom Beluck. He is charging you with violating his equal rights to the Constitutional Amendments. You have to appear in court to answer these charges."

"I don't remember this inmate. Is this really going to go to court? What am I supposed to do?"

Secretary Leasy replied, "Don't let this worry you John; this has been happening a lot. Inmate Beluck is also suing the prison system including the Commissioner and the Superintendent, along with you. I have already contacted the Inspector General's office. They will be sending an investigator down to talk to you. I will call you when they get here."

Walking back to my shop and passing through Center Gate I noticed Sergeant Jim Work standing in the doorway. I approached him about the summons.

Work remembered the inmate. "I'll never forget that one; he made a big stink about being locked up."

"I guess I better go and read this summons," I replied.

I went back to my shop. As I waited for inmates to report to work I went through my files on inmates that we are required to keep for ten years, and pulled the Beluck folder and reviewed it. It was true. He has been on parole for over a year now. I could not understand why he would want to chance returning to prison stirring up trouble and telling lies while on parole.

A week later, I received a letter from the Inspector General's Office. They acknowledged receipt of the summons and the complaint from inmate Beluck. The letter read:

> We will, pursuant to Public Office's Law S17, be representing you in this litigation. We must determine that you are within the terms of the statute, which provides for indemnification by the State and representation by the Attorney General, provided you acted in the discharge of your duties and in the scope of your employment. And that the damages did not result from a willful and wrongful act of gross negligence.
>
> We will undertake an investigation to determine whether the acts involved in this action are within the statute and will inform you as soon as that investigation is completed. During the investigation we will take whatever steps are necessary to protect your rights in the litigation.

I enclose herewith the Complaints and Questionnaire. In order to determine whether representation is appropriate, and, if so, to prepare your defense, it is necessary that you do the following.

The Questionnaire was fifteen pages long, approximately one hundred questions to be answered true or false.

The first three said it all.

> 1-Mr. Pecchio had deliberately and repeatedly written fabricated disciplinary reports on this inmate. (False)
> 2-Mr. Pecchio caused this inmate to be punished because of his abuses and illegal acts. (False)
>
> 3-This kind of abuse and mistreatment is prohibited by the United States Constitution, and thus, because of the Institutional Adjustment Committee, misconduct and racial discrimination, this inmate has been deprived from having his equal rights to Constitutional Amendment, when Mr. Pecchio called me a "Nigger." (False)

I finished the report and returned it to the secretary. I felt very reluctant dealing with Inspector Generals and other high-ranking State Officials. I had been approached by them too many times and knew how they operated. While waiting for the Inspector General to contact me I studied my reports and was prepared to answer all the questions asked by the court's attorneys.

Within a week, the Inspector General came to interview

me. We talked about the charges against me. Halfway through the conversation I remarked, "I reviewed Beluck's records and wondered why this inmate was not transferred to another facility because of his bad disciplinary record. Isn't that mandatory?"

"He was going to be paroled so administration kept him here, I guess," he said.

A few weeks passed. I finally received notice from Central Office Inspector General. "John, the lawsuit and charges have been dropped against you. The inmate never showed up for the hearing. So take it easy, it's over."

If the charges and lawsuit were dropped, and I was never questioned, accused, or asked to attend a court hearing, then why was I put in the State Legal Book for calling an inmate a Nigger?

The State Legal Book documents all lawsuits by prisoners who file charges against state employees working in a prison system throughout New York State, showing the nature of the charges and settlements. Now all prisoners throughout the system can have access to this book by requesting it at the law library within the prison compound. Inmates will then use the information against employees, using the same charges, in hopes to make it stick.

I locked up an inmate in my class for refusing to work. He just sat there and said, for all to hear, while waiting for the guards to come and pick him up for a Keep-Lock, "If you called me a Nigger I would kick your a**." He was escorted out of my shop. More was to come from this prisoner.

111

Inmates have a saying: "What goes around comes around!" In other words, if you set them up, they will set you up. To overcome the fears of prison backstabbing you must always be in control of your shop. Keep busy, be a good listener, and always keep a professional attitude while working around inmates. What helps to keep a well-run shop going is a good work schedule, constant improvement of learning skills, cleanliness, visual aids, and giving the inmates a positive outlook. Inmates will have less time to get into trouble if they are kept busy learning.

An inmate working as a porter on my floor in Shop 5 was not allowed into my shop to clean, or enter without my permission. His name was Ted Post. When the officers were given extra duties to patrol all the shops in his area, both up and down stairs, inmate Post was often left alone. A guard could only be on one floor at a time. He could wander in or out of the other shops and down stairs at will. Carrying a broom in his hand, pretending to sweep as he walked, he could visit inmates throughout the areas. The broom was a good weapon if he needed to defend himself.

Post was a slick operator. He would always show pictures of himself with the notorious gangster John Gotti, posed with guns in hand. He had an inmate friend, Bill Jazz, working in my shop. Post knew he was not allowed in my shop without permission. He kept trying to warm up to me by offering to take the garbage or clean up the shop.

At the time I had been told by security that too many inmates were being caught with all types of leather projects from my Shoe and Leather Shop. I warned my inmates that if any more leather was stolen from this shop I was going to stop the leather project and do only Shoe Repairing.

This did not set too well with them. They liked making leather projects for their families. When it was time to clean up and turn in the tools that afternoon, I noticed Post talking to Jazz through the screen fence that separated the shop from the hallway. I gave it a few minutes, waiting and observing. An inmate, Larry Combes, came over to tell me that Jazz was putting leather into garbage bags and giving them to Post. Later the bags would be taken to the garbage wagon past the Center Gate. Jazz and Post had a leather business going.

I set a trap and caught them both stealing leather projects and locked them up for stealing state property, being out of place and interfering with an employee doing his duty. When the officers were coming to pick up Jazz and Post the shop's officer searched them down. The officer found a steel pipe strapped to the inside of Post's leg. It was later learned that he was going to hit another inmate for stealing his leather.

I wrote my disciplinary report; put the evidence into the contraband box with both reports witnessed by the two Correctional Officers, Jim Mase and Iven Mclean. My boss and Sergeant Ted Marks were witnesses on both reports. The shop's officer, Plaza, wrote up inmate Post for carrying a pipe on him.

After Post was Keep-Locked he made up a story about me and sent it to Captain Bill Yates, stating that: "Mr. Pecchio is harassing me. I overheard Mr. Pecchio say, 'I will get that inmate Post. He's a baby rapist.' Mr. Pecchio is playing inmate against inmate and he is bringing in food and liquor for the inmates."

Lieutenant Bill Rollons came to my shop and told me that he had a letter from Captain Yates to investigate the charges that Inmate Post made against me. I got very upset and wanted to press charges on Post for false information and harassment. Lieutenant Rollins said, "Take it easy John, these are the new changes from Central Office, and we have to follow through." I had to put my story in writing again about what happened when I Keep-Locked Inmate Post and gave it to Lieutenant Rollins for a report to Captain Yates.

Inmate Post got word that I was pressing charges against him and wrote a letter to me saying, "Dear Mr. Pecchio: I know you want to file charges against me. If you go into court with this, and I lose, it will hurt my family to see me get more prison time, and this will put my mother in the hospital. The only reason I lied was because you locked me up. You have kids, Mr. Pecchio. I am still a young man, twenty-five years old, and have made mistakes. All I want to do is go home to my family."

I gave this letter to Lieutenant Rollons and the case was dropped. Post went on parole. Six months later, Lieutenant Rollons was passing me in the prison yard one day and told me

114

Post was shot six times in the head by the Mafia and died.

CHAPTER 18

SHAMS, CHARADES AND CIRCUS

In March 1983, three inmates doing "life in prison" for murder escaped from the Elmira Correctional Facility. All three had a good institutional record and qualified for a transfer to the Honor Block.

It was interesting to learn how the escape took place. These trusted inmates had contacts that got them a hacksaw blade then simply cut through the steel bars in the window facing the front of the prison. There is a guard on duty about forty feet away facing the prison. The inmates waited until there was a heavy snowstorm and escaped through the window. The guard never saw them.

Six weeks later, two of the inmates were caught. The third was caught three years later while robbing a bank of $13,000. Ten years later, one of the three inmates who escaped tried it again and was caught. All three were incarcerated in a maximum-security prison that is supposed to be heavily guarded. How many more crimes they committed; while on the run; no one will know for sure. All three were put back into the Guardhouse, appeared in outside court and received more time on top of their "life" sentence. Each one was transferred to a different prison.

Central Office leaders set up training programs for

employees, teaching them to maintain a relaxed security atmosphere when supervising inmates. The training programs are very close to the same training received from the Army in preparation for entering a war zone. Part of that training consists of the riot procedures, handling chemical agents, weapons and surviving attacks. I never heard of any special war zone training to prepare society for released prisoners. Central Office, very candidly, will try to make unions and employees believe they are upgrading the working conditions in the prison system. After all the training and efforts the staff puts into implementing these procedures, you may think you are going to be safe, but that is not so.

Protecting oneself against a surprise attack from a convicted murderer, who is very muscular and has no remorse on his prey when he is ready to attack or kill, is an experience one does not forget! The employee under attack, if possible, tries to get to a phone and call security for help. Some Correctional Officers and civilians working in certain areas of the prison can carry a walkie-talkie radio when they are available, but they always seem to be in the repair shop. It is hard to talk on a radio when a prisoner is attacking you.

Prison rules give an edge to the prisoner. State Prison rules do not allow the employee to protect or defend himself when the prisoner decides to stop his attack and sit down, or just pauses for a few seconds. You have to make a decision as to whether that pause means he is not attacking you any more. If you continue to attack or defend yourself, then the issue becomes "How much use of force was necessary to protect yourself?" You could be out of a job if you do not have the right answers or witnesses.

Every freedom in prison will be taken advantage of. Taking down the screens in the visiting room was a big mistake. This was, for sure, an accident about to happen. Without the screens there was too much personal contact, which permitted the passage of drugs and sex.

Governor Mario Cuomo was against the death penalty for twelve years and was supported strongly by religious leaders. George Pataki, who favored the death penalty, ran against him and won.

Just before the election, Vice-president George Bush was praising Cuomo, telling the American people that, for the past twelve years, the Governor was against the death penalty and a Federal Crime bill would help New York State. The Governor's record in fighting violent crime was good, but crime rates were on the rise.

Commissioner Thomas Gold was in charge of all the State Prisons in New York State while Cuomo was in office. He told the public, "Life in prison without parole is better than the death penalty. Prisons are safe. Life without parole is a penalty that potential killers fear worse than death. That is why killers like Thomas Grasso have begged to be put to death rather than end their lives in prison."

Frivolous politicians play with power and decision making with a flip of the coin.

Gold was telling the American people that capital punishment did not deter crime and that we must respond with strong laws firmly and effectively enforced. He said how could anyone pretend that capital punishment will make us safe? During Gold's administration thirty-eight new prisons were opened that housed 40,000 inmates.

Thomas Grasso was sentenced to twenty years to life for murdering an eighty-one-year-old man because there was no death penalty in New York State at the time Grasso pleaded guilty to a previous murder a year before. That time it had been an eighty-seven-year-old woman he had strangled to death in Oklahoma City, where they do have the death penalty law.

Now, with a double murderer and states fighting to see who will keep him alive, Cuomo won a court case forcing Oklahoma authorities to return Grasso to New York State to serve his twenty years to a life sentence for the first murder. Grasso endorsed Oklahoma's bid to execute him.

Cuomo and Gold could not get anywhere with the Grasso murder case and fought it until both retired. The new Governor, George Pataki, and acting Commissioner of New York state prison systems now had to deal with murderer Grasso.

New York State had reinstated the death penalty as Governor Pataki promised. The first thing Pataki did was to keep his promise to let Grasso be executed in Oklahoma City. Death penalty opponents said a pardon might be the only way Pataki could send murderer Grasso back to Oklahoma City where he faced execution for murdering an elderly woman in Tulsa, Oklahoma. Pataki had already ruled out a pardon for Grasso.

E. J. McMahon, a spokesman for Attorney General Dennis Vacco, said he could not disclose the strategies Pataki and Vacco were pursuing in the Grasso case. They believed that they have a very clear idea of what needed to be done, but they did not want to say what it involved.

Out in Oklahoma a spokesman for Governor-elect Frank Keating had said that Grasso's case would be dealt with immediately after Keating was sworn in. In a State speech Governor Pataki repeated his pledge to make sure Grasso is executed and he intended to send Grasso back to Oklahoma City to receive the punishment he deserved. Grasso, who was thirty-two years old, was put to death by injection four years later in Oklahoma City.

Since justice has been served, and with Grasso dead, his ex-wife Lana Yvonne Grooms has been charged with helping with one of the murders. However, at the time Grasso was alive, the case was delayed filing a murder charge against Grooms, fearing that Grasso would decide to fight his execution and be expedited back to New York State. To date I do not know what justice did with Grooms for her involvement in one of Grasso's murders.

Now that the death penalty is reinstated in New York

State lawmakers still find it hard to execute a murderer because of some quirks in the law. When a crime was committed before the death penalty was reinstated, the criminal got life imprisonment.

Can you imagine keeping a mass-murderer like Richard Speck for years in a prison, protecting his rights and pampering him? Speck brutally stabbed and strangled eight college students to death. One victim who got away from Speck had witnessed everything and testified at his murder trial.

Speck was having a good time in prison because he ran free in the prison population by dealing drugs, and having inmates catering to him.

On national television one day, I was watching a program, "Rivera Live," and the segment on murderers was interesting. It showed Speck shirtless, with very large breasts, which were believed to have come from silicone shots. He was bending over in a cell spreading what was said to be powdered cocaine on a black inmate's upper thigh, licking and snorting it from the knee toward the inmate's penis. In prison, this is called, "Doing sexual favors for pleasure, money or just cigarettes."

How could this be taped right under the noses of the prison authorities in a maximum-security prison? And Speck's explanation why his breasts were so large was that he was flabby in his chest!

Speck finally died twenty-five years later from a heart attack. The question remains, how did Speck smuggle drugs into

121

a high security prison and what did prison officials ever do about it? The cover up and the rest of this story will never be known.

In February of 1984 the death penalty was in effect in Pennsylvania. A murderer, Steven Duffey, who was thirty-three years old at the time, killed a nineteen-year-old woman by stabbing her thirty times. The prosecutors said Duffey forced the girl into a restroom at a restaurant, stole her money and a watch, and then stabbed her repeatedly as she pleaded for her life.

Lawmakers stalled the death penalty on Duffey for ten years. This was costly to taxpayers and the state's budget that always goes past its due date, paying interest to keep the state programs running until the budget talks are approved. The scare tactics used on state workers always comes up at budget time, which leaves a lot of stress on employees, not to mention the prison system, who wonder if they have a job or not. But Duffey's nineteen previous execution dates were halted during that time and finally the Governor signed Duffey's death warrant.

Courts, law enforcement and politicians always prescribe to keep Americans safe on the streets. How does one define "keeping Americans safe?" John Gotti was a mob boss who murdered anybody. He was nicknamed "The Teflon Don."

Salvatore Gravano, a murderer nicknamed "Sammy the Bull," was one of Gotti's gang members who turned informant on him.

Gotti now wanted a new trial, stating that Gravano lied and had killed twenty-one people, not nineteen. Gravano never got the death penalty. He informed the law and got Gotti. Gravano did confess that he only killed nineteen people. He made this statement to Federal law enforcers in a court of law and in front of twelve jurors.

Gravano's testimony against Gotti, combined with Gotti's own secretly taped admissions, produced a racketeering conviction against him, along with conviction of other crimes and murders he committed in the "Mafia."

While the trial was in progress the prosecutors told the American people that "they believed Gravano's statement was true about Gotti. He would never lie in court."

How could the courts allow a mass-murderer like Gravano to go free? They exchanged one murderer for another, getting the more notorious criminal Gotti. The Lawmakers made a deal with Gravano. If he helped them get Gotti, when the trial was over, he would be put into a witness protection program and become a free man! End of story!

In October of 1993, in Santa Rose, California, a twelve-year-old girl was having a slumber party when Richard Allen Davis broke into the house where the three girls were playing and abducted Polly Klaas. While Davis was abducting Polly, he very nicely told the other two girls in the room to count to 1,000 and then Polly Klaas would be back to play with them. That never happened. Davis was arrested and two months later led the police to the body of Klaas.

Davis had a long criminal history and had spent more than

fifteen years in prison for six convictions ranging from burglary to assault with a deadly weapon. The list goes on, including armed kidnapping and sexual assault charges involving at least four women. One attack occurred when Davis was on probation for burglary. After the arrest in that assault he was sent to a mental hospital for testing. He walked away with flying colors and soon attacked another woman in her home, beating her with a fireplace poker. However, that never stopped prison parole boards from allowing Davis to go free. He was released only three months before he killed Polly Klaas. What was the parole board thinking when they allowed him to go free? How could they think he had changed?

When the X-rays were released twelve-year-old Polly had only six baby teeth when she died. You could hear Davis laughing throughout the whole videotape.

He told authorities "with a smile on his face" how he masturbated twice a day while thinking of the victims he had killed or assaulted.

Davis and his attorney, Collins, sat at the defense table. One of the girls, who saw Davis taking Polly Klaas from the room, was on the witness stand when she pointed to Davis as the abductor. Two other witnesses in the room were face to face with Davis and identified him as the killer. Prosecutors had witness after witness that stated that they saw Davis in the neighborhood weeks before the kidnapping of Klaas. Davis' attorney admitted to the jurors that Davis did kill the twelve-year-old Polly Klaas. This should have been it. The jurors should find Davis guilty of murder and he should receive the death penalty. Now, three years later in 1997, Davis, sentenced for capital punishment, is still waiting execution.

The prosecutor described serial killer Joel Rifkin during his trial as "The Killing Machine." He was responsible for the deaths of seventeen people. They were sexually assaulted in his truck after which he strangled them and then dumped them in a wooded area. For all of these deeds the court gave Rifkin life imprisonment.

Jeffery Dahmer admitted killing at least sixteen men and boys. He chopped and dismantled bodies, boiled them, and even ate some parts of the bodies. After admitting that he strangled, dismembered and cannibalized them, the courts found Dahmer sane and sent him to prison for sixteen life sentences. An inmate did what the court should have. He killed Dahmer.

More recently, the Oklahoma City bombing resulted in a loss of 169 lives. More than five hundred people were injured. The evidence compiled by the F.B.I. proved beyond a doubt that Timothy McVeigh and Terry Nichols were guilty. McVeigh got the death sentence and Nichols got off easy. He got life in prison. Years later, after appeals filed in court, McVeigh lost and was sentenced to die by lethal injection. That final day cost the taxpayers $13.8 million. And the last appeal, which was carried out just before his death sentence, cost the taxpayers more than $147,000. As for Nichols, on the other hand, one state wants him tried for the death penalty while the other state wants him to serve his life sentence first. I feel sorry for the taxpayers paying these bills and also for the victims' families.

Colin Ferguson had used a Semiautomatic weapon while standing in the middle of a train, shooting at random into the crowd, killing six people and wounding nineteen others. There was no death penalty in New York State at the time Ferguson murdered these people. He knew this and, without any remorse, committed the murders.

There were nineteen surviving victims who testified that Ferguson shot them. About twenty other passengers gave their statements about what they saw when Ferguson was doing the shooting. It took thirteen months to bring this man to trial after he was arrested.

Ferguson, who defended himself, first planned to challenge the jury system of Nassau County as unfair to blacks. He asked the county court Judge, Donald Belfi, to subpoena President Clinton and former Governor Cuomo of New York State as trial witnesses. If that was not enough, the thirty-six-year-old Ferguson had 1,200 potential jurors summoned to the court system and another 3,000 on standby to be summoned by telephone, if needed.

The court gave Ferguson $300.00 to mount a search for the unidentified white suspect that he blamed for the rampage that turned out to be a lie. When all was said and done Ferguson was found guilty of the commuter train massacre. The Judge handed Ferguson the maximum consecutive sentence of twenty-five years to life, along with ordering him to serve a fifty-year maximum for the nineteen counts of attempted murder, two weapon charges and reckless endangerment. Experts viewed the trial as a sham, a charade and a circus. How else can it be described?

CHAPTER 19

INMATE TROUBLE

One day in August of 1982 while working in my shop on a Monday morning, an inmate, Carl Cruz, came in escorted by a correctional officer. He asked to have his shoes fixed. In the meantime he was trying to get the attention of another inmate, Bill Merkey, working at his bench.

I examined the shoes and told Cruz they could not be fixed. He then insisted I have Merkey make him a pair. I told him, "That is not the way we do things, you have to go to the dressing room." I gave him a receipt for a new pair of shoes and he became argumentative. The guard had to calm him down. During the commotion Merkey came up to us and asked if he could make Cruz a pair of shoes.

"This conversation is over, Merkey. You get back to work," I replied.

The officer motioned to Cruz, and said, "Let's go. Thank you, Mr. Pecchio."

Cruz remarked, "We'll see about this."

The officer told Cruz to stand by the door and came back into the shop and explained to me that Cruz was on strict medication for a mental illness and had to be escorted all over the prison.

When they left I went over to Merkey and asked, "What

was that all about, are you in trouble with Cruz?"

"Sort of, but I will handle it."

"Do you owe him money? Is that why you wanted to make him a pair of shoes?"

He looked down and kept on working, saying nothing. That was his answer. I said nothing more and continued my rounds instructing inmates.

The next morning as I was walking through the yard with another civilian, Bill Hanson, who had just started working that summer, I could hear a window opening and an inmate yelling.

"Pecchio, kiss my a**." The window slammed shut.

Hansen said, "It's terrible how inmates can say what they please and get away with it."

"You have to learn to live with it. Besides, it's hard to catch him, with two hundred windows facing the yard, all looking the same," I replied.

For the next two weeks, when I walked through the yard where it was very quiet early in the morning, I heard a squeaky window opening and the same voice shouting, "Shoemaker, your mother sucked my d***." Then the window slammed shut.

This was getting to me. One morning, Larry White, the Tailor instructor, was walking with me and, hearing the verbal attack asked, "You want to catch that idiot?"

"Yes," I replied.

"Meet me here tomorrow morning before we walk through the yard and I will show you how to catch him."

The next morning White and I met at door thirteen facing the yard. He told me, "You walk out first and when you get about twenty feet, stop and wait until I get under the windows of the cells where the inmates can't see me then continue to walk with me."

Sure enough, a window opened, and the inmate started calling "shoemaker." Just then White stepped back and pointed to the window of the inmate's cell. "Oops," the prisoner said as he slammed his window shut.

"There's your man, the eighth cell from the front of the block, four tiers up," said White.

I was so relieved. I walked right into my boss's office and told him what I had been going through for two weeks and that I had located the inmate's cell. He laughed, saying, "I thought you'd be used to it by now. You've been here long enough."

"I want him put in the Guardhouse," I replied.

"For what? There are more than two hundred windows overlooking that yard. You really think you can write up an inmate on hearsay without seeing him face to face? He'd make a fool of you at the disciplinary hearing."

"You're right; I will go to the block and confront him."

"You better tell security. That is their job," he replied.

I left and contacted security. They also said, "You can't lock up the whole block. Go up there and talk to the inmate. If you think you have the right one, tell the block officer. He'll know what to do." I did just that.

I approached the cell and, sure enough, it was Cruz.

"You are the one who has been yelling at me every morning. If I ever hear another word and name calling from you I will make sure you do hard time," I said.

"Okay, you got me, I am sorry," he replied.

I left and walked over to the correctional officer and told him what was happening. He said, "I overheard Cruz telling an inmate about a week ago that you would not make him a pair of shoes and he was going to get you. I checked his records and talked to the brass. They said, don't worry about it, he's on strong medication and will be locked up until his transfer which is tomorrow." I just walked away shaking my head.

About a month passed. The correctional officer who escorted Cruz all over the prison was walking through the yard at the same time I was. He mentioned to me, "You remember that inmate Cruz who was calling you all those names? He got stabbed in another prison and died."

"That's always the way most of those loud mouth inmates end up," I said.

It was budget time again so I requested new machines. I put in my order as I do every year and, again, Bono, my supervisor, replied, "There is no money in the budget."

I was out front on my lunch hour a week later and noticed superintendents from various prisons throughout the state standing in the waiting room getting ready to tour the prison. A man leading them on the tour came up to me and asked, "How is your mother?" To my surprise, it was Jim Bates, the Deputy Commissioner in charge of all the prisons in New York State. He was a friend of my family for years. For a short time he had worked at the Elmira Correctional Facility as I did. He then worked his way up to his present position. I said my mother was fine.

As we continued talking he asked, "Is there anything I can do for you?"

"Yes, get me some money for my new shoe machine."

He replied, "I'll get back to you, I have to run for now, take care." He then proceeded to tour the Facility with the Superintendents.

A few weeks passed. Bono called me into his office and said, "Who do you know in Central Office? They gave me money for your new equipment." I told him about my conversation with Bates, who said he would help me.

CHAPTER 20

SUPERVISOR TROUBLE

Bradley, Director of Education, was retiring and his successor was Fred Grace. Shortly after Bradley retired, Bono followed in his footsteps and retired. His replacement was Larry Caffe.

Grace was a small man, very inexperienced with vocational training, and depended on Caffe who had been a Vocational Instructor for about seventeen years before he applied for the Vocational Supervisor's job. He too was a short, heavyset man, always scheming and playing jokes on everyone. Over the years we worked side by side and I always considered him a friend. Later I was to question this friendship.

It was mandatory by Central Office rules and regulations that you must serve one-year probation time before receiving a permanent position as Vocational Supervisor. It seemed that he would be a good man for the job with all his experience in the vocational department. While he was on work probation Caffe did not want any trouble from instructors working under his supervision that would make him look bad.

He would ask me personally to help him in solving some of the problems he was having with newer instructors. During his probation period I received the highest performance evaluation: "outstanding."

The year passed and Caffe became a permanent vocational supervisor. Within weeks he became very demanding, arrogant, and the type of supervisor who would lie at the drop of a hat. It was unbelievable! This man did a complete turnabout. His demands on instructor's work and performance were hard to follow.

One hot day in August the inmates were restless and I was sitting at my desk doing paperwork while the inmates were in front of me studying and talking at the table. No machines were running and the tools were all locked in my tool cabinet. Caffe came into my shop and up to my desk. He pointed his finger at me, "I am going to give you a performance evaluation now." His voice was very loud. You could hear him all over the shop. The inmates were silent and, along with other employees passing by, wondered what was up.

"Now?" I asked.

He yelled back, "Yes, now!"

It has been a ruling that when an instructor is going to be evaluated by his supervisor he is supposed to call a few days in advance to give the instructor an opportunity to set up some kind of program as a courtesy.

Caffe became more argumentative during the evaluation.

"Take it easy and cool down. Why are you shouting at me?"

That did it! He stormed out of the shop without saying a word. I immediately called his boss, Grace, and asked him to come over because Caffe was acting really strange. He said he would come over immediately.

While I was still on the phone talking with Grace, Caffe came hurrying back into my shop and in a deep voice told me to hang up the phone.

Grace was still on the phone and listening to the conversation between Caffe and me.

Grace said he would be right over. After that statement I hung up the phone and walked over to Caffe saying, "I had enough of this and I don't know why you are abusing and embarrassing me in front of everybody. What did I do to you? Grace is coming right over to see what your problem is."

He stood there for a few seconds staring at the shop and then turned and walked out the door.

A few moments later, Grace came running into my shop and told me that Caffe had slipped going down the steps and Center gate called for a stretcher because he needed medical attention.

I explained what had happened and Grace said he would take care of the matter but first wanted to check on how Caffe was doing.

As it turned out, Caffe was off for the rest of the summer and Grace, with the help of another instructor, filled in for him supervising the instructors.

In passing one day, Grace told me that he was looking into the situation I had with Caffe, but could not do anything until he returned in the fall.

During the summer things went smoothly. Caffe was not getting paid while off from work. He was on a ten-month calendar so if you do not work you are not paid and no sick time is available.

I knew when he returned I was in for a hard time. It reminded me of all those years working under Bono and Bradley. The nightmare was happening all over again.

I tried to explain this to Grace, about Caffe's vendettas and how he would be out to get me when he returned. Grace laughed and said, "Aren't you bending this out of proportion a little?"

I replied, "You don't know Caffe as I do; I worked with him for seventeen years."

The summer ended. Caffe returned to work and began to request inmate reports on the ones I had Keep-Locked. He would always request that the reports be in by the close of the day.

His vindictiveness was out in the open. Even though administration knew and was well informed there was nothing they could do because the supervisor's word was gospel.

The union was caught in the middle. Caffe and I belonged to the same union. The union leaders could not take sides and face being brought up on charges for not representing both Caffe and myself. He should have been dropped from the union when he became management, but his membership continued as long as he paid his dues. And he did keep them up.

When Caffe saw another instructor associating with me he would make sure to find something wrong with that person's performance and would try to get him fired. I know of two instructors, friends of mine and on probation, who were his victims. He made it look like something else was the reason for his or her dismissal, knowing that no one on probation can challenge a supervisor's report.

The union was only a formality, but was the only source I had to challenge Caffe. If you went to the department heads with a complaint the first thing asked was, "Did you file a grievance with the union?"

Caffe had a reputation of doing as he pleased. He would put things into your personal files or in your school folder for his Boss to see and you never received a copy. Union leaders have mentioned to me that there is an agreement between the Union and the Department of Corrections that a copy of any reports going into a personal file should be given to the employee.

I decided to check my personal files, but was discouraged by the clerk from seeing them. She would say things like, "You have to go through your boss first, I am too busy right now and cannot take the time to get my folder. Could you come back in a couple of weeks?" Checking your personal file is not complicated. They just get it, place it on a table and you sign for it. This should take about thirty seconds. I came back in a few weeks and finally got to review my folder.

Anyone with authority can put in or remove papers from

your folder when they see fit. In my case, another personnel lady brought to my attention that she had witnessed Caffe putting papers into my folder and removing some as well. After reviewing my file, I did find papers removed and others added. I had my old copies, but none of the new ones. I immediately questioned the reports with the personnel clerk who claimed she knew nothing about any changes. I knew she was a good friend of Caffe and was not about to violate her trust in him. I filed a union grievance and went through Hell with Deputy Superintendent of Programs to prove that they were false reports replaced by Caffe.

When there is a problem at one of the prisons, Central Office sends an investigator to check on the situation. The first thing the investigator does is pull the personal file to assure that it is up to date.

One time I remember being investigated from one of Caffe's set ups. I filed a union grievance and wrote to Central Office about his capricious nature. Inspector General Lester Mann came to interview me. My union steward, Tim Robinson, was present at the time. I could not get a word in and was frustrated listening to Mann discussing my case. I stood up and asked if he wanted to hear my side of the story. He said, "I already have your story, go sit in the waiting room and I will send Robinson out to call you back in a few minutes, I want to talk to him alone." Before I left I noticed that Robinson sat through the whole meeting and could not say a word.

I got up shaking my head, went out and waited. About ten minutes later Robinson came out and said, "John, the Inspector General knows what a temper you have, so keep it cool. Let's go back in." As I walked back into the room I was thinking, *the Inspector General did all the talking so how did he come up with* "I have a temper."

As the meeting continued the inspector started right in on me saying, "You have a temper, don't you?"

I finally spoke up and said, "If you were in my shoes and were constantly setup by your supervisor, and had given documented proof of his abuse of power towards me, and nothing was done about it, wouldn't you be mad as Hell?" He said nothing. As I continued telling my side of the story and finished he sat there silently and kept on reading my folder.

Finally, after ten minutes, he said, "I will get back to you after I have a chance to investigate this matter."

Later in the week I was cleared of any wrongdoing, and I never heard a word about Caffe or how he would be disciplined. Robinson did not know any more than I did.

One thing that I learned from these meetings is that the inspectors use their loud voices, finger shaking, and intimidating remarks to scare you into feeling guilty, whether or not you are guilty. When you try to explain how fraudulent these reports are it makes you look guiltier.

On several occasions I wrote up Caffe for filing a false report on me, but nothing was done to him. He was hitting on everybody he could, trying to make a name for himself; you could see that his authority went to his head. Instructors' complaints were out in the superintendent's office. You would think that he would back off and lay low, but not him! Even after his bosses warned him, he kept on coming, and making the vocational department a living Hell.

Caffe knew how to manipulate the new officials and play up their ideals. He knew that these officials wanted no trouble to show up in Central Office, making them look bad for not settling the problems at agency level. So they did their best in backing up Caffe's horrendous decision-making marathon against his challengers.

Caffe knew how to bend state rules and twist them to his advantage. He was good at this. Caffe's reputation was, by now, well established. As a one-man army he believed he was indestructible. He could care less who knew what he was doing.

I had seen earlier evidence of his deceit. When Caffe was an instructor like me, the prison had a shut down and we were ordered to search for weapons and contraband. All the Civilians, assisting guards, had to work out of title. Caffe disliked working out of title as so many others did. During these searches we had to feed inmates, sweep floors, search blocks and shops as though we were security guards.

This particular day, Caffe and I were sweeping the top gallery of G-Block as two officers paired up and were searching inside the cells. An inmate, right in front of Caffe, put a glass jar full of white paint on his bars to let the officers see it. Caffe was leaning on his broom handle looking around making sure nobody was watching. He then took the broom handle and pushed the jar off the bars back into the inmate's cell. Broken glass and paint were all over the floor. The inmate started yelling at Caffe, calling him an a**hole. Officers came running out of the next cell when they heard the shouting. The inmate very hurriedly told the officers how Caffe purposely knocked his paint off the bars. Caffe just looked around as if nothing had happened. When the Correctional Officers confronted him (Caffe) about the paint-jar he said, "I would never do a thing like that," and smiled. The inmate kept on calling him dirty names and a liar. The two Correctional Officers had no choice but to take the inmate to the Guardhouse. As the Correctional Officers were escorting the inmate to the special housing unit Caffe was laughing and seemed to enjoy what he had done. I told him, in no uncertain terms, how I felt.

Walking back to our shops we said nothing to each other. I could not get over what he had done to the inmate. You learn not to be a snitch or volunteer your opinion. No one was hurt. I was never asked about the paint incident and I said nothing about it to anyone, but if I were asked I would have told the truth.

Now I was under his supervision and the object of his deceit. I had a problem about working out of title. I took my inmates to recreation that day and continued working in another area of the prison as ordered. The next morning I saw Caffe and told him, "Working out of title was not teaching inmates a trade." That afternoon he came right up to the shop to discuss the problem and demanded that I work out of title. I took a long look and then I said, "I remember when you were an instructor like myself, how you hated out of title work. You even put in a union grievance."

He said, "That was then and this is now," and left.

The next morning Caffe called, telling me to report to his office at noontime. When I got there I noticed his boss, Grace, sitting in the chair by his desk. Caffe said in a stern voice, "Here is your counseling letter. Sign it!"

"You have to be kidding," I said.

The report read that I refused to work out of title. I told them that I had never refused to work out of title. I signed the report as ordered, but did so under protest.

I then said to Caffe, "I heard you had a tape recorder on you when you did my last performance evaluation. That is illegal and is against state policy." He said nothing, got up and walked into his other room, and copied the counseling letter I had just signed.

Grace, keeping an eye out for Caffe, whispered to me, "What tape recorder?" But before I could answer him Caffe came back into the room with copies of my counseling letter. Grace sat there in silence. On the way out of Caffe's office I told him that I was going to write a rebuttal to the counseling letter.

The taping, which had taken place, was during my

previous evaluation by Caffe. I had no idea it was being made at the time. An instructor had confided to me that he had heard my voice on a recording regarding a performance evaluation when he walked in Caffe's office one day unannounced. This Instructor had hesitated to tell me about it because he was on probation and if Caffe knew he had heard the tape, and talked to me, he would be set up and fired. I assured him I would not pursue it any further and not to worry.

As I was walking back to my shop I was thinking about the counseling letter and how Grace never said a word and was more than willing to back up Caffe's counseling letter. Standing by my door leading into the shop, I noticed the Electric instructor Jim Backer's shop was also locked because he was off for the day. As I looked toward the Radio and TV shop, Instructor Paul Boar's door was shut. I knew inmates would be turning out for the noon program so I called Boar's shop to see if he was in the back room. There was no answer. Just as I hung up I saw Boar on his way to his shop. He just gave me a wave from the hallway and kept going.

I unlocked my tool cabinet to get ready for the afternoon inmates and noticed a six-inch screwdriver was missing from my shadow board.

I locked the cabinet back up and called Caffe to report the missing tool. He said, "Give me a missing tool report, and then call security." He then hung up. I waited until all my inmates reported for roll call and told them of the missing tool and asked

143

them to be seated. I knew all my tools were accounted for when I went to Caffe's office at noontime. I called security and in a few minutes a Sergeant and seven correctional officers came in and started a thorough search of the shop while inmates sat at the table in the front of my shop. When security finished searching the shop and each inmate they took all of them to recreation for the day.

I was writing my missing tool report when Grace came into my shop that afternoon.

"Caffe called and told me about your missing tool. Did security find anything?" he asked.

"No, I had all my tools accounted for before I went to Caffe's office to get that counseling letter and when I returned, the screwdriver was missing from my locked tool board cabinet."

Grace never questioned me when I told him all tools were accounted for when I left that day for Caffe's office. All he said was "write a missing tool report and make sure the Watch Commander gets it at the end of your shift." (Watch Commander is head of security and in charge of the prison when the Superintendent is absent.) I complied with Grace's orders.

Boar's inmates left about an hour earlier. He locked up his shop and came right to mine. "What happened?" We sat down and I told him the whole story.

He told me that he also had gotten a call from Caffe that morning telling him to report to the Special Housing Unit (Guardhouse) and fix a TV, but when he got there the correctional officer knew nothing about a TV not working. He then called Caffe and told him that there was no TV to be fixed. Caffe replied, "That's funny, they must have made a mistake. Go back to your shop and get ready for the afternoon inmate's turnout," and hung up.

It did not take Boar and me long to figure out what Caffe was up to, but it was impossible to prove, especially with all the support he had.

Boar and I continued talking. It was very convenient for Caffe to have Grace as his witness when a tool came up missing from a locked tool cabinet. Obviously, Caffe sent Boar on a wild goose chase and the only other shop on the floor was the electrical shop, and he was off for the day on sick time. So the whole floor was completely empty at noontime. Anyone could have taken the tool from the tool cabinet and not be noticed.

I was trying to think who would help Caffe pull this off. It came to me that it could only be the Small Engine Instructor, Larry Sneeks, who was always in Caffe's office, doing out of title work for him without complaining. He was never in his shop teaching like the rest of the instructors and would always get outstanding performance evaluations. Caffe not only rode with him every morning but also had gotten him his job with the Department of Corrections.

Then I remembered, while in his office at noontime during the counseling session, Caffe was not wearing the leather key holder he asked me to make one day at the prison. "His keys were missing." He only had three keys hanging from his belt loop when Grace and I watched him unlock his desk. He always had at least thirty keys on two rings that he carried daily. For years I watched and remarked to my old boss, Bono, about all those keys he had to carry every day. All these keys were for all the vocational shops and tool cabinets. Caffe never let those keys out of his sight. He very well could have lent them to someone else.

The key room officer, Mike Boler, was a good friend of mine. When I turned in my report to the watch commander that day it was late. I then turned in my keys and asked Boler, "Did Caffe turn in all his keys when he left?"

"Yes, all thirty-two of them," he said.

All keys to your shop are picked up each morning and must be returned before you leave the facility at anytime, and are always recorded by the officer in the key room.

Driving home that night I was thinking, a missing tool from a shadow board that has a heavy padlock could not go unnoticed because of the outline of each tool painted on the board. Your eyes become trained to spot a missing tool in a second. The only way the tool cabinet could be opened was with a key or crowbar.

The next morning at about 7:30 A.M., I opened my shop as I do every morning. Right there in front of me in plain sight, sitting on a sewing machine, was that missing screwdriver. I could not believe it. I knew that all the people searching could have not missed it.

I immediately called Grace and told him that the screwdriver had turned up and how strange it was lying right on the machine in plain sight. I know how security went over the shop with a fine toothcomb and could not find that screwdriver.

He said, "Good! You must have overlooked it. Call Caffe and let him know."

I asked, "Will the missing tool report be removed from my personal file?"

"No, it will remain on your file for record keeping."

That ended the conversation. I stood there thinking that Caffe knew all the time what would happen and this was to be just another mark on my file. I called Caffe and told him how strange it was that the screwdriver showed up after everyone had left for the day. He said, "Someone needs glasses. It was overlooked. Be careful next time," and he hung up. That ended the story of the missing tool. No way was I going to pursue it.

CHAPTER 21

CAFFE OR ME

As time passed inmates' demands were becoming harder to challenge. The constant rejection from administration leaders rambling on every time an inmate was disciplined was appalling. Also, the devious methods and flourishing attitudes of my supervisor's use of power was devastating to others and me.

One day Boar and I were sitting in my shop during the lunch hour, as we did every day. He expressed his concern about not receiving a performance evaluation at the end of his probation period from Caffe.

Then he told me, "I know Caffe is keeping track of every move you make and he knows I eat lunch with you every day." He continued, "I could tell by his remarks, the way he answered my questions, when I asked him about some paperwork I needed. His remark was, 'See your eating buddy Pecchio, he will help you.'"

"Do you think he will try to make trouble for me?" asked Boar.

"I would not put it past him."

After lunch Boar went back to his shop. I knew he was feeling bad and worried. I was standing by the door waiting for my inmates to report for programs when I noticed Caffe coming up the steps. He walked right by my door and never

148

acknowledged me. He hurried into Boar's shop and a half-hour later walked by my shop again as he was leaving the floor.

That night Boar and I left together at the end of our shift. He showed me a letter that Caffe gave him, written by the Superintendent. It said that his probation period was up and he had a low rating while on probation, which was an automatic dismissal from service. Boar was finished at the end of his shift that day. He tried to file a grievance with the union, but that too was no good. When you are on probation you cannot file a grievance against any department head. It was plain and simple. Caffe's performance evaluation on Boar got him fired. Boar was known to be a good, responsible worker. He was fired because he was my friend.

Right after Boar was fired Caffe started to come down hard on me again. I was very upset with him and disgusted with the department heads backing every move he made against me. No way was I going to let him get to me. I was prepared to challenge him at any point and time. Whenever he made a remark or wrote some derogatory remark on my job performance I would rebut it. I felt that sooner or later someone would see his sick attitude and abuse of power and put a stop to it.

He could be shifty. There were rumors that Caffe was being questioned about his attitude toward employees by management. To make an impression on management Caffe started writing encouraging reports to his staff. Right after all the instructors worked out of title again he wrote a memo to all instructors, thanking them. The letter read: "I want to thank you for the cooperation and effort put forth this past week during the facility shut down. Your enthusiasm, willingness to cooperate and lack of complaining makes it a pleasure to have such a fine staff to work with. I feel the Vocational Staff contributed and accomplished a great deal during this period. Thank you, again." Within a week he was back to his old self, abusing his powers.

Before he became a supervisor permanently he had given me an outstanding report that read:

> 1-Instructor has a good understanding of educational goals of our Department. Each student is assigned specific job assignment daily. Class is under control.
>
> 2-Instructor has designed his course around the employability profile for his trade. Task sheets are directly related to the profile. Training aids have been constructed for students' use.
>
> 3-Instructor has incorporated shop safety into the rules for the shop. Work areas are free of obstruction and safe work habits are taught and practiced.
>
> 4-All records are kept up to date and submitted on time.
>
> 5-Shop organization is well planned and organized to make maximum use of training time.
>
> 6-Instructor achieves respect of students by teaching at their level. Individual and extra instruction is given to students that require it.

7-Instructor has utilized his students in performing many maintenance jobs for the institution. These jobs have been professionally performed and demonstrated the instructor's knowledge of the trade and his ability to teach students.

At the end of the report he recommended further personal action and training and development activities. Caffe, his boss Mr. Grace, Director of Education, and Mr. Johnson, the Deputy Superintendent of Programs Services, who is not only over Caffe and Grace but is third in charge of the prison, signed this performance evaluation.

Within a year's time Caffe tried to drop my performance evaluation from outstanding to unsatisfactory. That report said:

1-According to the employee's weekly maintenance report, work cooperation with other Facility disciplines is being done; however, this employee had never called this writer to obtain prior approval to perform maintenance work as he has been instructed to do. The employee's rating on this standard is rated effective, but needs substantial improvement.

2-This writer never received a request from this employee about inmates' previous experience. As this is now the only shoe shop left in the department, it is very possible that there have been no inmates claiming previous experience; therefore the employee is rated effective in this report.

3-This employee was directed by the writer during an inspection of his students' progress reports to make certain specific changes. To the progress reports that reflect an accurate record of instruction given, i.e., progress reports by this employee only reflect one or two days' instruction for a two or three-month period. The amount of instruction reported ½ day period for an individual inmate is excessive. The hours he reported on the progress report are not consistent with the period inmates. I rate him Unsatisfactory on this task.

4-Employee did not produce any of the requested records to this writer; however, during the midterm evaluation his folders were found to be current. This employee is rated effective on this performance standard.

5-Student progress reports reflect that inmates are given safety rules to read and sign and that they have also received instruction on several machines. All of this is reflected on the day the inmates were assigned. The discrepancies were pointed out to this employee and he was directed to correct them. Student progress reports received in the shop show that the employee did not take the corrective action he was directed. The employee is rated effective, but needs substantial improvement in this standard.

6-During the midterm evaluation I checked the employee's records. It was evident that there were inaccurate records of inmates' attendance and inmates' class hours. I gave the employee a copy of the standardized attendance sheet. The employee refused to produce one and refused to answer my request. There is considerable evidence that this employee has falsified maintenance reports that are turned into the Vocational Office weekly. This employee is unsatisfactory on this task.

7-Employee has task sheets or job cards listing tools and material for task. The employee has met performance standard on this task.

Recommend personnel action and/or training and development activities: Service Training for all instructors should be conducted in their respective fields. Central Office should schedule training seminars for each trade discipline. This evaluation was rated effective, but needs substantial improvement.

This bad performance evaluation was witnessed and signed by Caffe, Grace and Johnson. These same department heads signed and witnessed my outstanding evaluation just a year ago. Now rumors were going around the facility, that Caffe had put me from "Outstanding" to below minimum in only one year.

A correctional officer told me to read the Baton next week. This was a monthly booklet printed by correctional officers for staff to read. It read:

Honorable Mention, our candidate (Caffe) for this honor is a deserving person. He has the ability to take outstanding people and, in a short time, turn them into barely effective people. But then, on the other hand, can take people from Watkins Glen, Montour Falls (Caffe's hometown) or even a personal friend or relative and, in the same short period, make them outstanding. You must admit, it's a little hard to understand when a teacher goes two or three years without a class (Caffe's friend, Instructor Sneeks) and still be rated outstandingly. The next question is what does a teacher do if they don't teach?

I worked under Johnson and Grace for years. They are

the reviewers of all performance evaluations written in the education department. For seventeen years I had never received a bad performance evaluation until now. How can these two men aid and condone a perpetual liar like Caffe by signing this appalling evaluation? This not only shows the abuse of power being implemented here but how administration leaders stick together, always covering up for one another.

About 90% of the instructors working under Caffe's supervision were so frustrated with his vindictive attitude they wrote up a petition against him and had a meeting scheduled with Deputy Superintendent Jake Daniels. He was second in charge of the prison. I was not in that group. I had my own grievance against Caffe and challenged him myself.

The Caffe situation prompted Daniels to send for an investigator from Central Office to see why so many employees, and some Department Heads, were having problems with him. When the investigator was interrogating Caffe he played dumb, as usual, acting as though he had done nothing wrong and did not know why so many employees hated him. He shifted the blame onto his bosses, saying he was "just following commands and procedures." As usual, Central Office bought Caffe's act and backed him up.

In the meantime I had my union grievance in to remove the bad evaluation, and another one to be removed from under Caffe's Supervision. The union representative, Robinson, was reading the bad evaluation I received from Caffe. He could see how ludicrous it was and said, "It is just a plain case of harassment." He then wrote to Grace requesting a meeting at once. Here is his letter:

> 1-Over the past few years I have received numerous complaints from employees concerning Performance Evaluations. Last week Mr. Pecchio had a complaint about his Performance Evaluation. After reading Mr. Pecchio's evaluation it is my opinion that a serious discussion is urgently needed before the Performance Evaluation becomes a total farce.
>
> 2-Inconsistent administration of performance tasks, standards and ratings.
>
> 3-Timelessness of evaluation.
>
> 4-Failure of administration to follow guidelines as established on the Performance Program and Rating Forms.
>
> I am requesting that this meeting be held as soon as possible.
>
> Because of the above I am requesting a Labor-Management meeting between you and the three PEF Union Stewards covering employees in the education program — Mr. Hess, Mr. Walsh and myself. There is a possibility that the top Union man of our region, Mr. Taka, would also attend. I would like to address the following general areas of the Performance Evaluation system of employees in educating implementation of the Performance Evaluation System.

Two days after Robinson wrote to Grace it was sent to

Johnson, who handles all the first-step union grievances. Johnson's note in response to me:

> Reason - an alleged problem with Supervisor. I will be on vacation the next few weeks. I would like to address your problem upon my return. Until then I would hope that you would keep a low profile.

While waiting for Johnson to return from vacation Caffe knew about my grievances against him and how I had to keep a low profile until Johnson returned. He felt that if I were removed from his supervision he would be humiliated. Caffe wasted no time in working his plan. He got the new superintendent, John Mork, involved, and thought with Johnson away he could do this. I did not know at the time that Caffe was on good speaking terms with Mork and had Mork convinced he was doing a good job supervising.

Inmates were always listening when Caffe approached and knew how he was out to get me. Inmates knew that all my misbehavior reports went to Caffe first.

Right after Johnson left I had to Keep-Lock an inmate, William Hims. He was determined to push me into locking him up. Two weeks before the Keep-Lock, Hims requested to be transferred to paint class, but was denied. He schemed up a plan and used me to get out of class. He started to provoke me in front of fifteen other inmates who were sitting around a table while I was having a shoptalk. He became a real threat to security, and I had to lock him up.

The report went right to Caffe. He interviewed the inmate and convinced him to write to Superintendent Mork. Here is the inmate's letter:

> I have a problem with one Mr. John Pecchio of the Shoe and Leather Shop. I've been written up and locked up twice for so-called things I said and did. Mr. Pecchio is a liar. He has written up false reports on me and I will not tolerate this harassment any further. It can be dealt with on a man-to-man level or it can be dealt with on a savage level. I don't need this kind of trouble and I am sure you don't want it either. So I hope you can handle my Keep-Lock report without further problems.

As expected, a carbon copy of this letter was sent to all high-ranking security heads. This was an unusual to do when writing directly to the Superintendent.

The life-threatening statements Hims was making in this letter were a real threat to security and to me, yet Security Officials and the Superintendent did nothing.

Within five days Mork wrote back to the inmate: "In response to your memo to me, be advised that I have forwarded this to Deputy Superintendent, Mr. Johnson for his action. You should be hearing from him or one of his staff sometime in the near future."

How convenient for Caffe, knowing how Hims' letter would go to Johnson and another letter would follow by the superintendent concerning this matter.

When Johnson returned from his vacation he had input from Caffe, Mork, and other inmates who were witnesses for Hims. The first thing Johnson did was to return the inmate's problem back to Caffe for investigation. Caffe favored the inmates rather than me and wrote down every lie the inmates were telling him, adding his own thoughts, and returned it to Johnson who forwarded the report and his remarks to the Superintendent. Well, you know how this is going to turn out.

I received a verbal counseling from Caffe and had to rewrite the report on Hims. I stuck with the same report and expressed how this inmate had a series of Keep-Locks in the Facility. I sent copies to all department heads involved. About a week later other inmates were interviewed by security and lucky for me I had one inmate who spoke on my behalf to Security.

In the end, the inmate won. They took him out of my shop and transferred him to the "Paint Class." There, within a week's time, he was locked up again. Administration then shipped Hims and his problems to another prison.

Johnson made a decision on one of my grievances: "This grievance was discussed with a PEF union representative at pre-first steps decision. Inasmuch as the grievance involved an evaluation on which a rating was "Effective," it is the option of this writer that there are no contractual grounds for such grievances. The supervisor (Caffe) was within his sphere of responsibility in completing the evaluation as it was submitted and we do not view the evaluation to be a form of discipline in any manner."

This was a good move on Johnson's part. He changed my report to "effective," and Caffe had to rewrite the report, but still left in most of his derogatory remarks. That report was not "effective" but it was Johnson's way out. He knew you could not file a union grievance on a report that is "effective." Again, the union had to rebut the report. After another meeting with Johnson most of the remarks were taken out of my report and it stayed effective (so I was told). That meant the report had to stop right there. The next step would have been Central Office. He did not want that.

In the meantime I was still waiting to hear from Johnson on my second grievance to be removed from Caffe. If he rejected that one the next step was Central Office and a Labor Relations man would come to the facility and investigate. It would then be an open meeting and the Labor Relations man would want some answers, not excuses from the department heads.

I knew Caffe was under a lot of pressure because department heads were getting tired of this. The only way I could get results was to keep the pressure on by rebutting every letter I received from Caffe.

Only then did Johnson tell Caffe to back off me. He did so for about two months while this grievance was in progress. Then it started all over again. Caffe wrote me up on some paperwork that he claimed I did not get in on time. I had no choice but to write to the Superintendent expressing a wish that he would put an end to this supervisor's abusiveness. Here is my letter:

Dear Mr. Mork:

I would greatly appreciate you taking the time to read the following "Evaluation and comments." Mr. Caffe is trying to get me to quit or else have me dismissed. I do not want to lose my job as it means more to me then just coming in and picking up a paycheck. I've written to Mr. Johnson, who is trying his best, but Mr. Caffe continues to come up with more and more half truths and lies. Unfortunately, knowing the system as he does, he can get away with this behavior.

Rumors were going around from the vocational department "how they dislike Mr. Caffe's methods and wanted to quit because of him." Putting inmates against staff, and staff members against one another, is detrimental to the harmony of the system and should be regarded as a serious offense. I feel that Mr. Caffe has done this to me. He tried, while Mr. Johnson was away, to scare inmate Hims with the loss of his parole.

I realize that you must stand behind your supervisors, but there comes a time when you also need to stand back and see what is really going on. Since Johnson cannot get Mr. Caffe to leave me alone and let me run my shop efficiently I feel compelled to speak with you about this matter.

"Respectfully yours-John Pecchio"

Neither Superintendent Mork nor any other of his staff responded to my letter. The only report I received was from Grace, who came to my shop yelling at me, "Why did you write to the Superintendent and not go through me first?"

I replied, "I don't believe you said that. For the last year or so you had access to Johnson's reports he wrote to Caffe and me. The Instructors' statements and copies sent to you told you about Caffe's abuse of power methods. All my rebuttals I filed against him, you received copies, and you never challenged Caffe's decision writing, or took the time to let me explain. Last but not least, your signature was on that bad evaluation I received from Caffe and you never questioned that frivolous report, even after you told me, "I ran a good shop." I hope that answers your question."

He changed his attitude and asked me in a soft voice, "Off the record, what did you do to get Caffe so mad at you?"

"Caffe operates with a very vindictive attitude and his personality has diminished to where he is like a little Hitler, trying to rule as he wants. I am sure that Johnson must have told you how he (Caffe) discredited Mr. Hall, the director before you, and had contributed, underhandedly, information to Johnson. The results ended up in Mr. Hall being transferred out of the facility."

"It can't be all that bad," replied Grace.

"The truth will come out in the end and then you'll see his other side." That ended the meeting. (At a later date and time

Grace finally understood Mr. Caffe's dark side and was willing to go to court on my behalf.)

While still waiting for the Labor Relations man to look into my grievance I became ill for a few days and, as a result, I had to go to the doctor for a check up. Unexpectedly, I ended up in the hospital for an appendectomy. Two days after the operation the doctor was checking my stitches and said, "You'll be going home in a few days. The stitches will be removed in about ten days and you should not return to work for at least three weeks from the day of surgery." I agreed.

That same day Mr. Lotus, a Vocational Instructor at the prison and a good friend, came to see me. During our conversation I mentioned Caffe and his horrible tactics.

His remark was, "He is the same and will never change."

Then he said, "Do you know an inmate Chilo who works in your morning class and works in my afternoon class?

"Yes."

He told me, "Caffe was trying to set you up while you're in the hospital and wanted him to write to Superintendent Mork and tell a lie about you."

I replied, "Caffe is a sick man."

"How do you deal with Caffe setting you up all the time?"

"It's very hard, but what really bothers me is how he keeps fooling his bosses and gets them to go along with him, even though they know he's wrong."

At Budget time Central Office, as usual, was trying to

take shortcuts and close programs, complaining there was not enough money in the budget. The previous year at this time Caffe tried very hard to have my shop closed and almost succeeded. I could have been out of a job. I did get my budget reports in on time. This year was no different. I needed to file my report right away.

I could walk and get around fairly well so when the doctor came in the next morning I asked him if I could go home as soon as possible. I had to convince him that I would take it easy until the stitches were removed. I asked to go back to work. He hesitated and then said, "Okay, on one condition: you do no lifting and stay off your feet as much as possible for at least another ten days." I agreed.

I returned to work and at my desk waiting for my inmates to come. Within fifteen minutes all my class showed up and welcomed me back. I proceeded on with the program, sitting most of the afternoon.

My tool clerk passed out projects and tools as I collected inmates' IDs. When all the tools were passed out Inmate Lento came running up to my desk saying, "Your boss, Caffe, wants to set you up and is going to call for me this morning. I don't want to go."

"What do you mean?"

"Caffe is out to get you and I don't want any part of it."

Just then the Correctional Officer came into my shop from the hallway and said, "Caffe is trying to call you and wanted you to get off the phone."

"I was not on the phone," I said.

While we were talking the phone rang. It was Caffe wanting to see inmate Lento.

Lento again said, "I don't want to go."

"Orders are orders; you'd better go see Caffe."

I thanked him for telling me what Caffe was up to and told him not to worry. As inmate Lento left, Inmate Chilo came up to me and spoke in a low voice so the other inmates could not hear him: "While you were off sick, Mr. Pecchio, I had to see Caffe about my pay in his office. He wanted me to help set you up and write to the superintendent, telling him that you lied on the Keep-Lock report you wrote on me before you got sick."

I told the inmate, "If this is true, put it in writing and give it to me tomorrow morning when you come to work."

"Okay," he said, and went back to his workstation.

I knew one thing for sure, if an inmate puts something in writing and signs it he will be leaving himself wide open for disciplinary action if he lies. I believe he was speaking the truth.

The next morning Chilo and Lento reported for work and handed me the letter I had asked for. I read it and was very upset. Caffe was trying to set me up all right and was going to use these inmates to do it. Chilo did most of the talking, telling me, "We want no part of Caffe's set up."

I explained to them that the only way for them to get out of this was to talk to another supervisor, or security.

164

"Okay, we'll do that," Chilo replied.

I immediately called Bill Blatt, another supervisor in Academics. I told him the story and he came right over. When Blatt arrived he took both inmates into the back room and talked to them for about a half-hour. When he returned he told me, "I have the statement of both inmates and will give them to Grace."

I knew how Grace favored Caffe so I called Robinson, the Union Steward, and told him the problem. He told me, "I need to call a higher official, James Taka, at the main office." He would get back to me.

Turning inmates against instructors is a real security problem. I called Lieutenant Jim Bloomer, who I considered a good friend and very conscientious person. I knew I could trust him. He came right away. I explained what Caffe was doing to me. He interviewed both inmates behind closed doors for about twenty minutes then, after the interview, Bloomer came out and said, "I have statements from both inmates and need to see Deputy Johnson."

That afternoon Bloomer returned, telling me, "I've seen Johnson and told him the story. He did not seem too upset about it."

Johnson's response was, "I know that Caffe and Pecchio are having a pissing match going on. I am working on it."

"I am sorry I can't do more for you, John. He is my superior," Bloomer replied as he left shaking his head.

"Thank you anyway," I said.

165

The next morning as I was working at my desk Caffe called. When I asked to see both inmates Lento and Chilo he said, "They will not be coming back today." When I asked him why? "He gave no reason."

The morning after that an inmate who was locked up next to Lento and Chilo came to my shop telling me both inmates were sent to Johnson by Caffe and had to talk about the problem. That is when Johnson locked them up for investigation.

"Could you help to get them released from Keep-Lock?" he asked.

"I would try, but it will be very hard because Johnson is a Deputy Superintendent, and is the boss."

I received a copy of the statement from Lento and Chilo, telling me about the conversation they had with Caffe, which read:

> I (Chilo) went to see Blatt at the school's third floor concerning my pay and was told that Caffe could help me since he handles all payrolls. When I got to Caffe's office we spoke about the payrolls, then he asked me if I'd been Keep-Locked by Mr. Pecchio.
>
> "Yes," I said.
>
> Then he asked, "Was it over bulls***?"
>
> "Yes because I refused to clean up with Lento."
>
> Caffe said, "You should write to the Superintendent about this and before you send it to him let me read it."

"I gave a copy to Caffe and he sent it onto the superintendent," Chilo said.

"Watch out to who you speak to because Pecchio has a lot of snitches," replied Caffe.

After reading the letter I called the blocks where Lento and Chilo were locked and asked the guard why they were locked up.

He said, "For investigation by orders of Johnson."

I knew what Johnson was doing. He was hoping the inmates would run scared and change their stories. That never happened. Now I knew why Caffe took them out of my class. He did not want me talking to both of them.

I was not about to take this lying down. I wrote to Caffe and in no uncertain terms told him to stop harassing me, that I had proof, in writing, how he wanted to set me up using inmates. I was going to send this letter and another letter to all department heads.

When I sent the letter to the superintendent I included a personal one about Caffe.

That personal letter read:

> I apologize for writing to you, knowing that you must be as tired of this as I am, Sir! I feel I must defend my job and reputation from Caffe's attacks, lies and set ups. I've already had a counseling letter removed from my personal file and my last performance evaluation, per orders of Johnson, had to be rewritten by Caffe because of his devious lies. I will challenge any rumors or

false statements made against me at any level. Sir, I don't want to see anybody lose his job. I'd rather change supervisors. "Respectably yours"

Of course, nothing was done and again Mork never replied to my letter, even after I sent documented proof, witnessed and signed by three other supervisors who interviewed the inmates and took their statements about how Caffe tried to use the inmates to set me up.

Grace talked to Johnson and found out I went to security and got statements from inmates. Grace came to my shop and was mad as Hell!

He said, "Why did you have to go to Lieutenant Bloomer? This is not a security matter."

I said, "Why did Johnson make light of it? He told Bloomer there is a pissing match going on with Caffe and Pecchio."

I continued telling Grace, "Caffe has been trying to set me up for the last two years and nobody seems to care about that."

I could see that Grace was not going to talk about the problem. He said, "I've got to go to a meeting," and walked away still angry. I never heard or saw the inmates again. They were transferred out of the facility. I was hoping it would help my grievance to be removed from under Caffe's supervision.

This whole thing, from start to finish, was just another cover-up by the faculty leaders. It shows how they stick together under any circumstances.

Johnson turned down my second grievance hearing. It went to the third and final step, the Labor Relations Board. There it was reviewed and a discussion about my removal from Caffe's supervision was held.

CHAPTER 22

MORE CAFFE DECEIT

I knew I had to check my personal file before I had the hearing with the Labor Relations Board if Johnson turned the second step down. This time I took Robinson, the union steward, along with me. That got the files in front of us in only two minutes. The first thing we looked at was the bad evaluation of Caffe that Johnson promised to rewrite for me. It was never rewritten! Reading further, we noticed a few more pages of misleading remarks that were entered by Caffe, and he even got other prison leaders that he had been priming behind my back to support him. I never received any copies. All the rebuttals I wrote against Caffe's performance evaluations and other derogatory statements were taken out of my folder. This for sure would have an effect on the decision against me when Johnson was ready to present it to the Labor Relations Board. We finished looking at the folder and Robinson's only remarks were, "We will see about this."

I could see that I was being set up again. This time I wrote a letter to Commissioner Gold and sent it by registered mail. Here is that letter:

> Mr. Gold, I request that a thorough comprehensive inquiry be made regarding the capricious nature with which the above-named individual (Caffe) executes the appointed position he presently holds.

The specific allegations are harassment, personal vendettas and a vindictive attitude. Many other Vocational Instructors, Security Personnel, and persons throughout the facility feel the same way and fear reprisal in the Vocational Department. I have mentioned, in writing, to the Superintendents down through the chain of command and the union about his abuse of power. I presently have a second grievance filed with the union and administration, but I am not getting any results at this level. "Information upon request"
Respectfully: Mr. John Pecchio.

About a month had passed and there was still no response from the commissioner.

Robinson called me one day and told me Johnson removed my old performance evaluation from my folder and replaced it with the new one as he promised.

I asked, "What about the other papers Caffe put in my folder without my knowledge. Will they be removed?"

"We will deal with that after Johnson makes his decision. If not, then we can talk about it at the Labor Relations Board hearing," he replied.

Caffe knew I sent a letter to the Commissioner against him. His reputation was at stake and he needed something that would sway the grievance board to his advantage. I knew he would try to stress his contaminated views on my next performance evaluation and needed a witness to back him.

I became suspicious when Caffe started coming to my shop three and four times a week. I questioned him, "Why so many visits?" He said that is my job. He would only come to other shops on an average once or twice in two weeks. On all of his visits to my shop he would wander all around, into my storeroom, checking and hoping to find something, and always finishing by talking to inmates at a distance so I could not hear him.

Then, after four visits, he returned to evaluate me for two hours instead of the normal fifteen minutes. I questioned him about his sudden visits and asked for time to prepare my class so I could visit with him. He became obnoxious and said, "You should be prepared for me anytime I come into your shop!" He started his evaluation anyway and asked me all sorts of questions about shop security, materials and record keeping. He then toured the rest of the shop on his own, talked to inmates, and left without saying a word.

That following week Caffe was making his rounds again. This time he had a witness, Jake Lamont, Superintendent of Industry, with him. He was a very easygoing person and well liked. As they entered my shop they noticed me talking to the shops' correctional officer in the hallway about ten feet away. Caffe gave me a strange look and then started talking to Mr. Lamont. I had complete view of my shop through a chain-linked fence and was telling the officer, "to be on the alert for two leather belts that were missing." I was done talking to the officer and then followed right behind them as they entered the doorway of my shop. They walked around surveying it for the possibility of moving my shop to another location, making room for a print industry shop.

The next day I received a counseling report from Caffe, explaining that when he and Mr. Lamont entered my shop they found me standing in the hallway talking to a correctional officer. It said I had been out of place and not giving my attention to the inmates. I had violated standard procedures.

He never mentioned that I had a complete view of the inmates at all times while I was there consulting the officer about my missing belts. As long as I was viewing my inmates this was considered standard procedure. He also never mentioned that I was talking about two missing belts. It was a set up and he had a witness.

He had also tricked Lamont into signing a false report about me. This letter was put into my files, very conveniently, before my hearing. I wrote my rebuttal letter and sent it through proper channels.

The very next day I was in the yard on my way out of the facility, talking to Lamont and told him, "You have been set up by Caffe."

"I don't want to talk about it," he said.

As we continued to walk I showed him the counseling letter he had signed with Caffe. He looked at it, stopped dead in his tracks, and noticed that Caffe had added a paragraph that was written after he had signed it. He then turned around and walked back toward Caffe's office.

The next day during my lunch hour I was sitting at my table eating lunch when Mike Ruler, a trusted friend from the agricultural class, came to join me. I talked about my counseling letter and how Caffe had gotten Lamont to sign it. He said, "I know about it. I talked to Lamont and he felt bad backing up Caffe against you. He was very angry when Caffe added a statement without his knowledge."

I called the union steward, Mr. Robinson, and he came to my shop, read the counseling letter, then went straight to Caffe's secretary and got a written statement from her. In that statement she said Caffe dictated the counseling letter for her to type. She had not typed in the extra paragraph after Lamont signed his copy; Caffe did that. Robinson gave me a copy of her letter. I was discussing with Ruler what the secretary wrote to Mr. Robinson about what Caffe did. Ruler's remark was, "You will get him fired for sure!"

All of this information was gathered and sent to the Superintendent, Deputy Superintendent, and the Union. It was passed around like a dish of cookies. Nothing was ever done to Caffe. Lamont never said too much when we passed each other in the facility. He would just nod. I knew he felt bad, getting caught up in one of Caffe's set ups.

A month passed. I was in the officer's restaurant drinking coffee with Robinson when he told me, "I have bad news for you. Your grievance to be removed from under Caffe's supervision was turned down by Johnson and the Superintendent."

"Now what?" I asked.

"It will go to the third and final step at the Labor Relations Board in Central Office and they will have a hearing with you. If that is turned down, then it is over. You stay where you are."

About a week later Labor Relation Board officer Archie McDougall came to our prison to investigate my grievance. When he reviewed my folder with Robinson he made remarks as he continued pulling report after report from my file saying, "That damn Caffe put this junk into Pecchio's file even after he was ordered to remove them."

That day McDougall filed his report and it was in my favor. He told the Superintendent and Johnson to take me out from under Caffe's supervision — immediately! They did just that! I was so happy that this nightmare was over. I gave up on wondering why the Commissioner never responded to me about my letter of complaint against Caffe.

Later Johnson wrote to the Director of Education, Grace. Here is a copy of the letter I received:

> In an effort to establish a good mix of programs here, and the fact that the shoe repairing trade has a questionable market value in the community, we are, at the direction of the Superintendent, after a conference with the Director of Vocational Education (Caffe), shifting emphasis from General shoe leather Vocational Program to Hobby craft and Leather Works.
>
> Within the near future, the building in

175

Leather Craft aspect of the present Shoe Repair will be integrated with a Hobby shop and Hobby Craft Program, which will be part of the overall Special Subject Component.

In Order to facilitate this change we are directing that it will be your responsibility, with the assistance of the Special Subject Supervisor, Mr. Norton, to establish guidelines, policies, and procedures for a Hobby Craft Program, including the resources presently available in the Vocational Shoe and Leather program.

You will be responsible for supervision of the Instructor currently assigned to the Shoe Shop. This program change will start immediately."

Mr. Fred Grace was now my boss and I never did work under the supervision of Norton as suggested by Johnson. I will say this about Johnson, he knew how to cover his tracks by shifting the blame on the shop's future and not because Caffe caused all the problems.

I could not believe it but two weeks later, after I was removed from Caffe's supervision, he sent me a trumped up counseling letter, still trying to make me look bad by sending copies to all department heads. I mentioned this counseling letter to Johnson and he did tell Caffe to back off. It was still put into my files and nobody asked Caffe to take it out. I responded to the superintendent in hopes that the letter would be removed from my file.

I titled it, ***"A final tribute to a Vocational Supervisor:"***

All of the bad letters and performance evaluations you have written about me only showed your vindictive attitude. They all have been proven wrong and were removed from my personal folder. I am not under your supervision anymore so please stop harassing me. I sent carbon copies to the same.

The superintendent's reply was:

I reviewed a copy of the letter you sent to Mr. Caffe and was appalled by the sarcastic remarks. I wish to inform you that I will not tolerate this type of behavior from you or any other employee at this facility. I suggest you continue to do your job and keep your sarcasm to yourself.

Carbon copies were sent to all department heads, and that included Caffe.

My response to the superintendent's letter is:

I respectfully apologize that you misunderstood my letter to be sarcastic and in poor taste. I've written and submitted through the chain of command several memos over the past year or so about Mr. Caffe's abuse of power and nothing was done or accomplished. I became frustrated and did not want another trumped up letter of this nature going into my file. It has been my firm conviction that there is a problem in the vocational department that required your immediate attention. "Respectfully submitted"
John Pecchio.

I felt I had nothing else to prove to anybody so I just sent the letter to the superintendent and the union. At the time I was writing to the superintendent all of the other vocational instructors were also unhappy with Caffe's methods and wanted out from under his supervision.

A week later, after I sent my letter to the superintendent, I got a memo from Johnson. "Per orders of the superintendent and for the best interest of the facility, Mr. Pecchio will be placed back under Mr. Caffe's supervision." I was disappointed and could not believe that the superintendent would completely ignore the decision made by Central Office's Labor Management to permanently remove me from Caffe's supervision.

I immediately wrote to the Superintendent expressing why I should not be going back under Caffe's supervision and asked the reason for this change. I explained that I suffered mental anguish and harassment from Caffe's supervision and was now under a doctor's care for my nerves. The superintendent ignored my letter! It was plain to see that he was determined to put me back under Caffe's supervision at any cost.

I filed another union grievance and this time it went right to Labor Relations, Archie McDougall. A week later he came to hear my grievance again. At the hearing that day he told me, "Don't worry and take it easy."

The following day he wrote a memo to the superintendent and Johnson, stating that any harassment of staff was improper and should be reported immediately. I was called down to the superintendent's office again and McDougall assured me that I would be taken from Caffe's supervision for good. This time the

Superintendent did not challenge his decision.

Needless to say, I was very relieved. I hoped this would be the last encounter with Caffe.

I stayed under Grace's supervision and received my first evaluation after six months. It was effective, well written and an accurate report.

A year had passed and I received a letter from the State Insurance fund:

> In February of 1985 you were hurt on the job while trying to help a Correctional Officer who was fighting with two inmates outside your shop in the hallway. When you jumped in to assist the officer you were hurt and put on compensation. While on compensation you were observed moving a refrigerator. We have a witness who signed a document to that effect. You were in violation of the compensation rules and will have to pay back eleven working days that you received while on compensation.

I immediately wrote back:

> "Under the Freedom of Information Act
>
> I was entitled to the name of the witness who
>
> signed their statement of controversy." "The only
>
> refrigerator I moved, on or about that time, was
>
> after I was back to work."

Within a weeks time, I received the signed statement, and to my surprise, it was signed by John Lumbo, the new Tailor Instructor and a good friend. He stated in the report that he talked to his immediate supervisor, Mr. Caffe, who encouraged him to file the report with the compensation board against me. Then it all made sense. Caffe was up to his old tricks again.

I immediately called Lumbo and asked to see him at my shop during the lunch hour. He agreed and when he arrived I asked, "Did you tell anybody I moved a refrigerator at your house when I was on compensation?"

"No," he replied.

"Are you sure?" I asked.

"I am sure."

I then showed him the statement he signed against me, and mentioned the paragraph, "how he went to his immediate supervisor Mr. Caffe." Then I continued, "Did Caffe put you up to this? Why are you setting me up now? I never refused you any help if you asked for it. "Is Caffe holding your evaluation over your head until you get past the probation period?" (If you don't get a good evaluation while on probation you're fired!)

At a lost for words, he read the statement saying, "This is a set up, I will get to the bottom of this." He then turned and walked very fast out the door mumbling.

As he was leaving I told him he had better get someone to help him. "You're in real trouble now."

After Lumbo left I went over to Jim Winkle's. He, too, was a good friend, and occasionally filled in for Mr. Johnson when he was absent. I showed him the letter from the State Insurance Fund with Lumbo's signature. Winkles knew of Caffe's reputation and went right to Johnson's office. The next day Winkle came to my shop and told me he had talked to Johnson and he was going to help Lumbo write a letter to the State Insurance Fund.

About ten days passed and I received a letter from the State Insurance Fund that read: "Gentlemen: Please be advised that State Insurance Fund removes its controversy, and reinstates its acceptance of the period February 1985 – March 1985 as temporary total disability casually related to the injury sustained in the course of employment in February 1985."

The first thing that came to mind was why was a copy of that letter sent to Caffe? It should have been sent to my new boss, Grace. I had not been under Caffe's supervision for a year.

Even though Caffe and Lumbo were caught red-handed and Lumbo confessed directly to Johnson about Caffe's setting me up nothing had been done to either of them.

A month later, after the Lumbo situation, I lost my wallet. It disappeared from my personal locker. I immediately reported the loss to security, telling them that in all my years of service I had never left my personal items lying around. They were always put under lock and key the minute I entered my shop. No one could get into my locker without a key. The only persons who had keys were Caffe and the officer in the key room. Caffe never gave the keys to my shop to Grace, my new supervisor. I had my suspicions how my wallet came up missing, but knew it was impossible to prove. I asked for new locks from the key room officer and got them.

The Inspector General came from Central Office to investigate my lost wallet. At a hearing I was counseled and had to sign a paper. A letter went into my file. No fines were implemented.

Grace was very upset with me. I asked him, "Why are you so mad at me for losing a wallet?"

He replied, "Because the Inspector General had to get involved."

I asked, "Why wasn't the Inspector General called when a couple of vocational instructors recently lost a hacksaw blade? Gasoline was missing along with ropes, and another hacksaw blade was found in the auto shop cars. All they got was counseling from their supervisor, Mr. Caffe. These items were dangerous and could be used in helping inmates escape, take hostages or start a riot. Isn't that life-threatening? I lose a wallet that was stolen out of my locked personal cabinet and all Hell breaks loose. The Brass interviewed me, wrote a letter for my personal file, and then summoned the Inspector General from Central Office to investigate me like a criminal."

"It's how you look at it," he replied.

In 1988 a new prison was being built in the Southside section of Elmira. It was to house the most dangerous prisoners in New York State who were locked in their cells twenty-three out of twenty-four hours a day. Central Office highly recommended that Mr. Caffe and Mr. Mork take a transfer to the new prison when it was completed that following month to prevent any further complaints, which they did! The head union leader told me later at one of our meetings that these changes came about because of Mr. Caffe's abuse of office. About two months later Mr. Johnson transferred to another prison as well.

Shortly after Mr. Caffe left the facility I started getting harassing phone calls to my home from someone who would disguise his manlike voice. This person would say things like, "I have your records a**hole" and "I f***** your wife and she sucked my d***," and then hung up. I did manage to get some of them on tape, but the calls stopped for about three months. Then after that my phone would ring about once a week and no one would say anything. I could hear someone breathing so I would just hang-up.

A few years later, after I was placed on disability for administration's failure to help me in a life-threatening situation, I met a friend I had worked with for twenty-five years at the Elmira Correctional Facility. He told me Mr. Caffe was the one making those sick and harassing phone calls. He heard that from a friend, who was under Mr. Caffe's spell at the time, and wanted to wait until he transferred out of the facility to tell someone. He expressed his feelings of regret about going along with Mr. Caffe's sick games and his abusive methods. Luckily it was my friend he told this to or I would never have been able to confirm who was making the phone calls. At the time I was undecided as to what to do. I did not want to lower my standards to Mr. Caffe's level. After thinking what a sick, foolish and immature thing it was to do from a grown man in his late fifties; I just considered the source and let it lay.

CHAPTER 23

DISCIPLINE DIMINISHED AGAIN

The new Superintendent, Matthew Buelow, was more than six feet tall and had a very abrasive attitude. He had very little knowledge of prison operations and was here because of a political appointment. Deputy Superintendent for Program Services replacing Mr. Johnson was Larry Smarts. He was a small, short man, with little knowledge of how the vocational department worked. Rumors had it that when he was transferred from his old job to his present job there was a sigh of relief. He originally came from Central Office's management department, accepted a job in the reception center, and later applied for his present job. It did not take anyone long to see he carried himself with an arrogant attitude.

The new Vocational Supervisor was Paul Branch, the Art instructor at the facility. He was an easy-going person, but was a company man. He was the same person who was involved with me during the investigation concerning the inmate who carried the $15 and nameplate situation. Mr. Branch and I were on good speaking terms; we let the past misunderstanding stay there. We did our jobs as professionals. In all honesty I had respect for the man and still do. As I said earlier, when you are on probation under the supervision of good or bad prison leaders, you better not cross them or you are out the door. He did have a lot of pressure from Mr. Smarts, his boss, and did handle it very well. He was always ready to help, especially when I was setting up my shoemaking shop, and for that I was very grateful. To this day, when we pass each other on the street we always speak.

Things ran smoothly for a while. Then one day Mr. Smarts decided to put me back under the vocational department without any explanation. My supervisor was now Mr. Branch.

The Superintendent and Central Office did not know about Mr. Smarts' change. It is a State policy that Central Office be informed of any changes in programs within the prison system.

Smarts' letter to me read:

> Effective immediately, Mr. Branch, Vocational Supervisor, will be Mr. Pecchio's immediate supervisor. Mr. Branch will be responsible for signing your time card, attendance records, approving your personal leave request and writing your evaluation. Please plan to attend all future Vocational Staff meetings.

This shows just how administration leaders at the Elmira Correctional Facility did as they pleased to cover up their mismanagement without notifying Central Office.

It was over a year since I asked to be removed from my supervisor in the vocational department. At the time there were so many people involved: Labor Relations Board, Central Office, Superintendent and other department heads. Smarts was well aware of my situation. He was one of the board members that makes decisions on which employee is taken away from supervisors. Now, under a new Superintendent, he was determined to do things his way.

Administration leaders removed me the first time from my supervisor (Mr. Caffe) in the vocational area. I was given a new title and was supposed to be put under another supervisor, Mr. Harry Norton, Special Subject's programs. Instead I was kept under Mr. Grace, the Director of Education. Now Smarts is putting me back into the vocational department under a new supervisor, Mr. Branch. My title is supposed to be Industry and work under Mr. Lamont, deputy superintendent of Industry. Mr. Smarts took full responsibility and tried to make it sound as if he was the only one involved in this transfer.

Under this new administration things were very loose. Too many changes in rules and regulations that favored the Inmates were being made. Under the old system, when a prisoner was assigned to a program he stayed there for thirty days and could not be taken out. Now, most inmates would remain one day to a week and were then transferred. When an inmate was interested in learning a trade he stayed longer. There were fewer security problems the old way. This fact did not seem to bother administration heads and the inmate was shipped out regardless.

A few years ago, when an inmate was locked up for a disciplinary problem, he got thirty days in the Guardhouse. Now, he received three or four days Keep-Lock, or none at all, for the same disciplinary problem. There were fewer discipline problems under the three-day rule. The inmates were, and always have been, manipulating the prison systems from day one. But now they have pushed the prison systems to the max. Prisoners understood the new rules better than most employees at all levels. The Security system was now questionable. The thirty days lockup in the Guardhouse for refusing to work was gone. Now, when locking up the prisoner(s), the repercussion from superiors was demanding and appalling if the misbehavior report was not in their favor. The only way you could feel safe with a misbehavior report was if a prisoner physically attacked you or if you jumped in when two or more inmates were fighting and you got hurt.

The new methods of discipline were the walking ticket. You were in constant danger. After the inmate was written up for violating a prison rule he was kept in the class or shop with that same argumentative attitude, leaving you in a life-threatening situation until the disciplinary board could call him. This could take days.

Central Office management was protecting the disabled inmates like special guests. Most of the severe cases should be in a special unit at the hospital and not in shops with tools and machinery, taking nerve medication where other inmates were constantly teasing one another. If anything happened to a disabled inmate and you could not come up with a proper written report you were reprimanded and received a counseling letter or you were fired.

These mentally unstable and dangerous inmates were always in trouble. If you got in their way and were stabbed by one, his defense was that he was mentally unstable to stand trial and under the influence of state drugs at the time of the incident. Central Office was demanding that we, as employees, must be prepared to handle this type of individual. The problem was we had no training and the only ones qualified were doctors and trained nurses.

The other prisoners felt rejected and isolated when attention was focused mainly on the disabled. The shop was in constant turmoil and major problems were developing. It did not take long for some inmates to use the disabled prisoners. They would bribe them for sexual favors and prompt them to carry contraband from one location to another, knowing that when caught they would get light disciplinary action. As many predicted, it was like a time bomb waiting to go off!

One of many examples I experienced was when Inmate William Folder was waiting to use a Sander finishing machine in my shop to complete his project. His wife was going to visit him and he wanted to give her the gift he had made for her. A disabled inmate, Larry Wetter, was using the machine. Inmate Folder was standing right behind him, waiting and shouting, "Come on Wetter, get off the f****** machine, you have been on it long enough."

Wetter replied, "Go f*** yourself. I will be finished

189

when I am ready," and continued working.

Again Folder replied, "You had better get off that f****** machine or I'll kick you're a**."

I could hear them arguing and I knew it was a matter of time before they would start throwing punches at one another. I went over immediately and tried to calm them down.

"What's the problem?"

"He is f****** around and won't let me sand my project," replied Folder.

I told Wetter, "Let Folder finish his project; he has a visit later and needs his projects to take with him. You can go back on the machine when he is finished."

Wetter slowly walked away and stood at attention behind Folder, staring at him with a tense look on his face. I thought it was over so I turned to walk back to the office. All of a sudden I heard a loud noise behind me and before I could turn around both inmates were wrestling on the floor and punching one another. The rest of the inmates in the shop stood watching and were very quiet. That is a bad sign. Most of the inmates were against the disabled ones from the start and were ready to jump in and help Folder. I could not stop both inmates from fighting. As I turned to use the phone to call for help I lucked out; the shop officer had just returned to his post and saw what was happening. He called for help and then hurried into the shop to take control. Minutes later, eight correctional officers rushed in and helped to break up the fight and escorted both inmates to their block for a Keep-

Lock.

I had to write disciplinary reports on both inmates and the correctional officer signed them as a witness. The next morning I was called down to see Sergeant Keith Bilmore at his office. He wasted no time in telling me to rewrite the misbehavior reports.

"I have orders from the Superintendent to make sure both inmates are transferred to another prison. They've been like a thorn in our side since they arrived here. Rewriting the reports is the only way to get them out of here; I'll help you to rewrite them." The reports were rewritten. They were not far from the original, but were detrimental enough to secure the desired transfer of the prisoners. Before the inmates were transferred they were turned out one day for their recreation time. Wetter got into a fight with Folder and cut his right eye and he had to have stitches. Following a disciplinary hearing the very next day, they were transferred out of the prison.

CHAPTER 24

ISOLATION

Inside these prison walls is a small town, isolated far from civilization. The existence and combination of sicknesses, hostility, confinement, dehumanizing survival methods and low self-esteem make it tough to rehabilitate any prisoner. It leaves one isolated and puzzled most of the time, wondering when the next outburst from an inmate will happen and who the victim will be.

Every year, millions of dollars go into the prison system and most of that money is spent for frivolous reform methods. These accomplishments look good on paper, but the question is why the State's prison system keeps building and demanding new prisons every year at budget time. What should be addressed is why repeated felons who have been paroled commit most of the crimes in society.

When the last time a taxpayer was informed about how much money was spent on prisoners' "medical bills?" You would be astonished.

New York State has an average of seventy prisons and is still building new ones. Each prison averages 1,500 to 1,800 inmates, and the all solitary confinement prisons hold about five hundred to a thousand inmates. A yearly cost for one inmate's medical bill, depending on the type of medical problem, averages

$500 to $10,000 plus; not to mention the average $30,000 per prisoner to keep him incarcerated for one year. The prison system survives on taxpayer money. What little the prison industry earns does not even cover the utility bills within them.

Why is it that at election time politicians come up with answers to straighten out the problems of the prison system and after election very little action is taken to correct the situation? It is a myth to say the system is working when documented proof appears on television, in the newspapers and on the Internet.

Incarcerated criminals depend on the prison system to make them comfortable, paying for their keep, education, and attorneys defending their rights. When they are let out of prison and society rejects them they return to prison and blame society for the crimes they committed. The paroled felon is like a revolving door that never stops turning: in one day and out the next.

Prison riots and escapes are on the rise, along with inmates committing suicide in their cells. With all the modern and sophisticated methods used for watching criminals twenty-four hours a day five or six inmates still manage to escape together at the same time in a maximum-security prison.

The system has helped prisoners become demanding. They are in control. Bodily fluids are thrown at employees and murderers are released or paroled to commit more crimes and murder again. When a rapist is released from prison he is required under Megan's law to register in the community where he is going to live. The court system protects the criminal. The lawmakers make the laws and the court enforces them. Now the courts in most cases tell the public that over half the rapists did not come under Megan's Law because they were in prison before the law was passed. The rapist gets a second chance in society whether he is registered or not. He can commit his offence once again, get caught, charged and once again can be returned to prison. He cannot be rehabilitated.

Now the system challenges the AIDS victims making them comfortable while they are incarcerated. Other diseases slowly spread throughout the system. The close contact and confinement, over which the system has little control, makes diseases of all kinds hard to isolate. Too many inmates have daily contact with each other. Sexual relations, contraband food wrapped in dirty rags to seal its identity is carried by inmates from one part of the prison to another and eaten by other inmates to help spread the problem.

The cells of most inmates are very dirty. Cells are connected to one another and items can be passed to the next cell by reaching through the bars. Candy is eaten and wrappers are thrown on the floor. Spilled sugar from beverages and cereal and opened canned foods litter the area. Even though there is a daily security check and inmates are written up for filthy cells security can only be in one place at a time. There is usually one correctional officer to cover four tiers, watch more than two hundred inmates in their cells and attend to the responsibility required for their jobs. All the debris on the floor attracts cockroaches, assorted bugs, and rodents. The cells need constant fumigation and the state has a special company coming into the facility at least once a month or sooner to spray the whole prison.

The drug and alcohol program at this prison leaves a lot to be desired. Very few inmates take it seriously and when they are released back into society return to drugs and alcohol and prison. Most of the contraband that comes into the prison comes from the inmate's family or personal friends who visit them. The visits are too loose. Screens were taken down many years ago and the close contact between the inmate and his companion always stirs up trouble. For example, when an inmate holds a baby it might have drugs in its diapers, clothing, or hair. Even though packages and visitors are screened there are many methods used to hide contraband. At times prisoners make homemade brews and the materials needed are smuggled from the prison mess halls. Yeast is stolen from the bakery and all other ingredients similarly collected to complete a recipe.

These are the results of loss of control and absence of discipline.

CHAPTER 25

NEW MANAGEMENT,
NEW PROBLEMS

Smarts' goal was to make an impression on Central Office and he would stop at nothing to do so. In this way he became unpredictable and dangerous. His title was Director of Program Services. He also outranked the correctional officers. He seemed very determined to catch his staff in the act of doing something wrong so he could write them up. On several occasions employees have complained that Smarts would hide behind doors or cabinets listening to conversations hoping to catch anyone in the act of saying or doing something that he could write a report on.

One of Smarts' pet schemes was to remain at the facility after a shift ended. He would unlock a shop door, check personal files and lockers hoping to find something incriminating. If he found anything out of the ordinary he would immediately put it on a report and then counsel the supervisor, writing him up for not watching his charges closely. He put an enormous amount of strain on prison employees.

Branch knew he had to keep a low profile and stay tucked under Smarts' wings because he was on probation for his new position. When it was time to evaluate the instructors Branch did a fine job. He tried to give seven highly effective evaluations, but Smarts rebutted his decision telling him, "Never give any performance evaluation above effective. Change them now!" This was against state rules and regulations in the educational department. Branch told me this because I was one of the seven classified highly effective. The program evaluation's system was set up well before Smarts took his new position. Effective rating could make the difference between keeping and losing your job, getting a raise in pay, or advancement in the prison system.

During the summer vacations, teachers and instructors took time off. Administration wanted some shops open to take up the slack so those inmates would not have too much idle time. If you wanted to work you could fill in for the shops that were kept open. Summer vacation lasted about eight weeks.

One summer Branch asked me to work the Officer's Mess Hall. I accepted. In this restaurant there was a full time Correctional Officer, Jim Mold. He was a heavyset man, in his forties, and had been working in the restaurant for the past six of his twenty years with the Department of Correction. After the first week I noticed that Mold was lax in disciplining inmates.

Every morning I reported for work at 6:00 A.M. to start my day. Before I entered the restaurant, on the floor in the main lobby, fresh baked goods, (doughnuts, bread, etc.) were dropped off by a bakery. I picked them up and carried the load into the restaurant.

For about two weeks things ran smoothly. I had a good idea about the restaurant's operation. Each morning, I worked at the counter serving coffee and taking breakfast orders from the employees. We had to do this for about an hour until the inmates showed up after turnouts. After they had eaten in the inmate's mess hall, they would then prepare breakfast in the restaurant for employees.

One day Mold came over to me and said, "Slow down; when the inmates come, let them do the work. That's what they're here for. You're here to supervise."

"Okay, I will keep that in mind," I answered.

The next morning I was pouring coffee for employees when the inmates started to report for work one by one. They came in and only four began to work when they entered while the other six hung out together in the back of the restaurant talking and drinking coffee. I asked Mold to get them working. His reply was, "They are slow, let's give them time." I let that slide and did not want to jump the gun, hoping they would do better the next morning. But the same thing happened the following morning. It was annoying and the other four inmates were getting upset because they were doing all the work.

By now I knew the routine and I was going to be ready for the six inmates the next morning. I was determined that they would not get away with any more nonsense. Mold was too easy, making it hard for me to discipline them. That was his job. He was the security officer.

That morning I stood at the counter serving coffee. The employees started coming in and it was getting busy. As usual, the same four inmates were working and the other six were still laying back. I went to the back where they were drinking and eating fresh doughnuts. I looked over at the heat lamp and noticed that they had the day old doughnuts under the heating lamp and were serving the employees those stale doughnuts and charging them for fresh doughnuts. This made me very angry.

I said to the six men, "This has been going on long enough. Every morning you six report for work and eat and drink while others do all the work. No more! Go to work or be Keep-Locked."

"We have to wait for the doughnuts to heat up before we can serve them," replied an inmate.

"Look, I know what's going on, and it stops here and now. Go to work!"

No one said a word as I turned and walked toward the counter. Slowly they began working. The officer's shift was changing making the restaurant busier. This was Friday, fish fry day, the busiest day of the week. The same six inmates were not working too fast, but were doing enough so that I could not Keep-Lock them.

I took an order over to the gas grill where one of the six inmates' jobs was to prepare and cook as he was given the orders. He was not in a hurry and always got the orders mixed up. I am sure he did it on purpose. I went over to talk to him and as I was moving the loaf of bread I noticed five or six cockroaches coming out of the plastic wrapper. The inmate just looked at me, smiled and kept on making toast with that loaf of bread.

I grabbed the bread from his hands and told him, "You're all done. Go sit over by my desk. I'll be there in a few minutes to talk to you."

"I am not going and will stand here until you tell me what's up."

Mold was standing right next to us, and said nothing. I shouted at the inmate and again gave him a direct order to do as I said. He looked at Mold and then slowly walked over to where I told him to go.

I threw the bread in the garbage and called for another inmate to continue cooking. I went over to the inmate sitting in the chair and told him, "If anything happens like that again, you're out of here. I want you to start washing the back room and when the restaurant closes for the morning, disinfect and mop the whole floor."

"Now?"

"Yes, now!"

He did so without giving me any argument. By now the shop was quiet and all the inmates were working at a good pace. When it was clean up time at the end of the morning shift four of the six troublemakers were taking out the garbage. Only one is required to do this. I became suspicious and hurriedly walked over to the wagon saying, "Wait a minute, I want to check that."

"Lay off us, we're doing our job," replied one inmate.

"One man is sufficient to take out the garbage, you other

three clean up."

They paid me no mind and insisted on taking out the garbage right then and there. As I started to counsel them again I noticed some clean garbage bags on the garbage wagon. I continued to look further and found the fresh doughnuts and fresh pies wrapped in clean plastic bags.

"What is this?"

"This is old food that needs to go to the garbage dump."

I began pulling the garbage off the wagon and noticed canned foods were also hidden behind the other bags. Just then two more of the same gang came over. All of them were standing, just staring at me, with mean looks on their faces.

"I've had it! You know this is contraband. You are stealing State food, refusing to work and are breaking the rules of this restaurant and the facility. You're all Keep-Locked," I said. I called for Mold, "Call Center Gate, these six inmates are going to Keep-Lock."

Mold immediately locked the cash register and came running over to me and said, "What's up? This is fish fry day; we need all the inmates we can get."

"Could I see you over by the counter please?" I replied.

I started right in on him. "Look! Cockroaches are coming out of the bread wrappers that we are serving to the employees. Inmates are putting the stale doughnuts under the heat lamp and selling them to the employees as fresh ones. All six of those guys are stealing food, taking it out on the garbage wagon. They are refusing to work, hiding the new fish under the old and every Friday, and heating it up to sell!   Call Center Gate Now"

There were about six officers left in the restaurant. Mold said, "That won't be necessary, we have six officers to help and we will take them to lock-up."

While I was writing misbehavior reports on the inmates four Brasses, one clergyman and the headman for Voluntary Service Program all came rushing in asking why we had locked up the inmates.

I explained the situation and they tried very hard to get me to write walking tickets, which meant the inmates would not be Keep-Locked and had to stay in the restaurant to work.

"No," I said. "They are locked up and going to stay that way."

I finished the reports and two of the Brass stayed back, signed them and took the reports with them as they walked out of the restaurant.

Mold got right on my case saying, "We need inmates, this is the busiest day of the week."

I picked up the phone and called Grace, "Is it all right to close the restaurant? I am short of help because I had to lock-up six inmates."

"What the Hell are you doing? This is Friday. Did you have to lock all six of them up?"

"Yes. Cockroaches are coming out of the bread bag and the inmate was still serving that bread to the employees." I went on, telling about them stealing the food and taking it out in the garbage wagon, and that they would not clean or disinfect the floors or wash the dishes in clean water.

"You got to be kidding. I will be right over."

A few minutes later Grace came walking in. I told him the story. He saw the dead cockroaches and said, "Let's close this restaurant and get it cleaned up."

I relayed the message to Mold, standing by the cash register. I could tell from the expression on his face he was not too happy. He just turned around, closed the register and as he was leaving the restaurant said, "See you later."

Within three days the six inmates were replaced, the shop was cleaned up and opened for business the following Monday.

The rest of the summer went smoothly. On the last day before I left, Mold said, "You did a hell of a job, John. Hope to see you back next year."

CHAPTER 26

SMARTS' CONNIVING

Vacations were over. That first day as I returned back in my shop Branch came to see me. He said, "I heard you did a good job in the restaurant. The only thing is, the six inmates you locked up were complaining to the Superintendent and he wants me to investigate the matter."

"I filled out all of the reports and the Brass signed them. So what's the problem?"

"You know how things are. Don't worry, John, you'll be all right." He took my statements and then left. All I did was to repeat what I had written on the misbehavior reports the first time.

Three days passed. Branch called me to his office to discuss the six inmates. What the superintendent said was encouraging. The inmates were shipped out of the facility because they threatened the superintendent with a lawsuit. Case closed.

The next day I was checking my tools at the end of the period and noticed a tool was missing. My clerk and tool man was Jose Mandez. He was a good worker and never gave me any trouble. He told me he had lent the tool to Mike Waldo, his friend, and someone had stolen it. He knew he was responsible for any missing tools. He and I were the only people allowed into the tool cabinet. I called Security and Sergeant Bill Ward came with four other officers. They searched the shop, patted down the inmates and took Mandez to Keep- Lock.

Smarts was making his rounds and heard about the missing tool. He stopped in my shop where Sergeant Ward and the officers were searching. Ward was helping me write a missing tool report to the watch commander when Smarts said, "Be sure you give a missing tool report to Branch."

I finished up and left about fifteen minutes later, taking a copy of the report and a picture of the tool to Branch, then proceeded to the watch commander's office. I left my keys with the Sergeant who was going to lock-up my shop when he finished. I filled out all the paperwork needed and followed orders when I left the facility.

The very next day Branch called me to his office and began counseling me about the missing tool.

"I went by the book. You signed the report along with the Sergeant and never said a word to me when I left yesterday. Why are you counseling me now?"

"Smarts is mad as Hell! He said you lost the tool and wanted me to counsel you. I do know you did right, but this is what I am ordered to do."

"Okay, I will write my rebuttal in hopes that it will explain my side of the missing tool. I'll send a copy to Smarts and you'll get a copy along with the others."

I knew how Smarts operated. He liked to have something

hanging over your head because it gave him power and was leverage to use against you if you wrote a rebuttal or challenged a performance evaluation.

This was my rebuttal letter to Smarts:

> Mr. Smarts, I appreciate your concern for the missing tool, but I did follow proper procedures. I would appreciate it if you would reconsider writing the counseling session letter. Mr. Branch made a statement to me about how upset you were for the way I handled the missing tool and you felt I showed no concern by leaving early. That's not true! You were in the shop when Sergeant Ward ordered me to write a missing tool report and you mentioned that I was to make sure Mr. Branch received one as well. I finished up with the Sergeant that day and he asked me for my key to lock-up the shop when he was done. I did just that and proceeded to Mr. Branch's office, then onto the Watch Commanders' office. Both said that I did well in reporting the missing tool. I did not leave the Watch Commander's office until 5:00 P.M. that night. I went straight home and never put in for overtime. So how could I have left early that day?

A week went by and Smarts never responded to my letter. During that time an inmate found the tool in his towels when he unraveled them and he returned it. He turned the tool over to the block officer; I was notified and got my tool back, but the counseling letter remained in my folder.

One day I received a letter from Branch, with copies to Smarts and Grace, telling me that my shop was going to be closed down soon and I was being considered for a job in Industry running the Shelter Work Shop. Now I understood what Smarts' plans were. I am not paranoid, but I experienced enough to know how the facility heads operate when they want to make unorthodox changes. This was just another ploy to get me transferred out of the Vocational Training department.

Branch knew about Smarts' plan for a long time and did not tell me. I found this out later when Branch told me how Smarts kept the pressure on him and he could not tell me.

CHAPTER 27

MORE BUREAUCRACY OVER COMMON SENSE

I was to keep the same pay rate under the vocational department and Branch was still my boss. Someone made the decision that I was to be supervised by both Branch and Lamont.

All the changing around over the years was frustrating. All this was because Caffe had a one-man army syndrome going. At first I was removed from Shoemaking and taken out of the vocational department, transferred to the Special Subject Program and given a new title, Hobby-Crafts. I was supposed to be put under the direction of Special Subjects Supervisor, but despite what Grace's boss told him to do he kept me under his supervision. After Caffe left I was put back under the vocational department again. And my new title was not a vocational item. Then I was transferred to Shelter Workshop, an Industry item, given a new title, but was to keep my original title shoemaking and still be called a Vocational Instructor. That too was not a vocational item.

I wondered how Smarts was going to cover up all these changes and make it look as if nothing was ever wrong. As it turned out Smarts succeeded and I was officially in the Shelter Workshop under the supervision of Mr. Branch.

I was always suspicious of anything Smarts did for me, especially when he wanted me transferred in the system. At one point in time, Smarts was trying to get Central Office to transfer me to another prison's shoemaking shop five hundred miles away. I had no choice in the matter. After going to Central Office's distributing center to be legally transferred to the prison where Mr. Smarts suggested I found out there was no such shoemaking shop that existed. The lady asked, "why are you here?" She informed me I was the only shoemaking shop in the prison system. After a long conversation we shook hands and I was sent back to the Elmira Correctional Facility. Upon my return to the facility I immediately confronted Mr. Smarts. He looked surprised and confused and said, "I will check on this mistake." He never did.

A low budget at the prison was just another way of getting you to take a transfer or be laid-off. Employees were afraid of losing their jobs.

Smarts again thought it was a good time to transfer me out of title again. He wanted me to accept another job within the prison. This was to be Mr. Branch's old job, Arts and Hobby Shop. The pay was four grades lower and I would have another new title. I later learned that he worked up a plan with his fellow workers in Central Office, asking them to back him up in getting me transferred. If this worked he could transfer me out of the facility under the new title because many prisons in New York State had this program.

After a lengthy battle by the state and the Federal Government funds were made available to the prison system from Federal funding. That prevented the layoffs and we employees were reinstated.

Now Smarts could not transfer me because I was permanent and all programs were to remain as is. But even though funds were now available Smarts was still determined to transfer me. After several weeks Smarts succeeded in getting my shop closed. If a vocational shop is terminated and they thought you were not qualified for any other position, "you were out of a job." When the offer came up to accept the position in the Shelter Workshop in Industry I had no choice but to accept it. I had about twenty-two years in and needed three more to retire.

I asked my Union for help. "Why was I going to Industry and working under the same title as a vocational instructor?" They were just as surprised as I was. Smarts was behind the whole thing. I was told that Central Office was never informed. It looked like it was all down hill from here. Little did I know that the worst was yet to come!

I knew nothing about Shelter Workshop. Inmates made paint brushes and paint rollers, which were sold all over the country. I was willing to learn. I put my nose to the grindstone and worked very hard to learn all of the functions of my new shop. As the months passed I made good progress and had the hang of things. I had learned about all the machines and how to repair them. This gave me an advantage over the inmates who broke them. It was also good for keeping up production and saved on repair bills. My gross sales were up in just a short time.

Lamont and Branch steadily gave me compliments on what a good job I was doing.

Branch sent me a letter thanking me for accepting the "Shelter Workshop" position. He said, "From your past work record and experiences at this facility I am sure you will do an excellent job in the Shelter Work Shop." Amazingly enough, Grace, who received a copy of that letter, was backing up Branch's statement.

At evaluation time Branch had no choice but to give me a "highly effective" report. Again, Smarts intercepted and told Branch to drop me to "effective." I questioned Branch and he said, "Sorry, but that was Smarts' order, not mine."

I understood the greed for power these Department Heads thrived on so I did not hold it against Branch.

I continued attending staff meetings because my title was still under the vocational program. At one of these meetings Smarts was telling us how pleased he was with our performances. His remark was confusing. If that was so then why was he afraid to give us a better evaluation?

After a few more staff meetings I became aware of the reasons why Smarts was being so nice. The facility was going to be inspected and he, along with other prison leaders, needed a rating of average or above to receive the type of accreditation they wanted. State Inspectors would judge the security of the prison, how well the academic and shop programs operated, neatness and cleanliness.

These inspectors were not connected with Central Office because they were a special group who operated on their own. Therefore no politics was involved with Central Office. I never saw the department heads so worried before. They were running around like chickens with their heads cut off and needed everyone to cooperate if they were going to get the job done. If Smarts could pull this off and get the prison accredited he would be highly praised by Central Office and maybe get a higher paying job. Now that administration leaders needed help and were determined to impress the inspectors the babying of prisoners did not seem so important. The leaders of the prison were going to make an impression on Central Office at any cost.

The rush was on and everybody did his or her part regardless of all the confusion. We were now giving direct orders to the inmates to clean and work in dangerous places, such as climbing ladders and hanging onto rafters twenty feet high to clean windows in the skylights and working with caustic materials that were dangerous to their health. If an inmate resisted working in those dangerous areas Security would say, "Lock him up!" That put the misbehaver's walking ticket on hold for a while. It was back to the old method of lock ups. (And there were many throughout the prison). Central Office was not aware of how the superintendent and his staff were disciplining inmates during the accreditation time.

The teaching staff, working with correctional officers, was as well organized as professionals. The prison received accreditation with a good rating. The first compliment came from Smarts. Administration held a party for the employees. Despite all we did for Smarts he continued to hold all teachers and instructors' evaluations to "effective" in performance even though we went far beyond our job description working out of title.

In July of 1990 Branch took off for the whole summer and Smarts worked part time. Grace was left in charge of all teaching positions in the facility. He needed a supervisor to help him in the vocational department and asked me to fill in for Branch until he returned in the fall. I accepted and had to work double duty keeping the Industry shop going along with the vocational office duties. At the end of the summer I finally received a "highly effective" performance evaluation from Grace himself.

The summer vacations were over and all the teachers and instructors were back to work. By now I was settled in and things were going well in the Shelter Workshop. One day the Fire Inspector, Jim Blakeman, came to my shop complaining that he needed a back door for a fire escape. I told him I would report it to my supervisors, Mr. Branch and Mr. Lamont. When Smarts received the request from Branch he turned it down. Blakeman visited my shop on several occasions to check for the fire door. It had never been installed and he did not push it any further. Since Smarts outranked him, Blakeman could not override his decision even though it was not up to standards with the fire-code book, which was written by the State fire inspectors.

I needed my small walkie-talkie radio repaired. This was a radio issued by administration and we had orders to carry it on us at all times. We used it to call Security for help when needed. It was also very helpful when you could not get to a phone. Smarts never had my radio repaired. At a later date, during a Labor management meeting, the subject of walkie-talkie repairs was brought up. Smarts was present and turned down the request saying, "There aren't any funds in the budget." What happened to the special budget that was always on hand for such emergencies that was never dropped? I knew that the Federal Government had a grant for the State Prison and the money had been received.

A week or so passed. Sergeant Mike Walker came to my shop and requested the wall between the shops come down because it was a security risk. I thought to myself, here I go again. I told him to see Smarts; after all I am not maintenance. Maintenance is over in shop 6. They had civilians who supervised inmates for that job. He went to file a complaint with Smarts, who outranked him. Walker told Smarts that he had talked to me. The wall never did come down.

I asked Mr. Lamont, now one of my bosses, "I have been working in this building less than a year now and this building is more than a one hundred and twenty-five-years-old. Why is "security" always asking me about fire doors having to be put in, and walls that must be removed etc.?"

He had a good answer: "Don't worry about it, let it go in one ear and out the other."

Not long after that, at noontime, my boss came to talk to me. He wanted to know "what all the fuss was about." He was telling me, "Smarts was very upset with me. He felt you were causing problems in this building by getting Security and Inspectors to renovate your shop here."

I'll be damned. "I did not want to renovate this shop. The fire inspector, Jim Blakeman, and the Sergeant, Mike Walker, wanted to." I went on telling him, "All I want is my Security radio repaired so I could carry it on me at all times." He would not talk about that.

His reply to that was, "To cover yourself you better write a letter explaining what happened with the fire door and the wall to be torn down. Send it to me and I will see that Smarts receives it again." I did as I was ordered.

Weeks passed and there was no answer from Smarts. One day Branch was in my shop and I asked him about my radio. He told me, "I have not received any response from Smarts. I'd leave it alone because something is bothering him. He's been turning down a lot of maintenance work and I don't know why."

Performance Evaluations were due again. I was told by Branch that he and Lamont agreed that I should get a "highly effective" rating. When the time came for me to sign my evaluation it read "effective." When I questioned Branch he said, "Smarts wanted to drop you back from highly effective that

Grace gave me."

Then I asked, "Why did Grace not speak on my behalf? He signed my 'effective' report."

He replied, "You know how that goes. Smarts has the final say on all reports, I can't challenge that, sorry."

I signed the report and shook my head. From that point on I made up my mind to ignore Smarts' evaluation syndrome. I had a couple years left and as long as I got effective I could live with that.

CHAPTER 28

INCOMPETENCE – BITTER AND SWEET

I was getting really deranged inmates in my class. The overcrowding of inmates at the facility left no other place to put them. All the shops and schools were in the same predicament. My shop did not specialize in a vocational learning trade so the unskilled were assigned to my shop at random.

I had two dangerous inmates working for me. Their names were Lester Taylor and Frank Cole.

Taylor was serving more than two life sentences for killing three people. He was a colored man with a shaved head, more than six feet tall, weighing over two hundred and fifty pounds, and very muscular. He did not want to be in my shop and he made no bones about it. He had a very loud mouth and was a very demanding individual. Most of the inmates despised him. Cole was a tall white man, more than six feet tall, straight hair down to his shoulders, weighing more than two hundred pounds. He was serving a lot of time for multiple crimes. His attitude was the same as Taylor's and he also was very uncontrollable. Both inmates did time at Southport prison in Elmira, New York, where the worst inmates are transferred from all the prisons in New York State. Southport rules are very strict. Inmates are locked up twenty-three out of twenty-four hours a day with one hour for recreation. Cole was there for several months and then returned to the Elmira Correctional Facility to continue serving his time.

I had been monitoring both Taylor and Cole and with their present attitudes I wondered how they managed to get released from Southport prison. I treated Cole and Taylor the same as I did all the others; I was firm but fair. I always gave the men coffee and when I could I brought in doughnuts and other pastries for all the prisoners. I had hoped this would send a message to them that I wanted tranquility in my shop, not animosity. Unfortunately, Cole and Taylor would drink the coffee and eat their share of pastries, but were not interested in conforming to the shop's rules and regulations. They were bound and determined to do things their way no matter how well they were treated. Both inmates felt that being in "Southport prison" (that incarcerated the most dangerous inmates in New York State) made them wiser and stronger men. Between the two of them they tried to overpower the other inmates by dealing and promising to protect them from other inmates.

As time passed the inmates were really getting sick and tired of Cole and Taylor's bickering. On several occasions I had to counsel Cole and Taylor about their behavior that was disrupting my shop. Once again; Cole and Taylor ignored my commands and both continued their bad behavior. I had no other choice but to Keep-Lock them again. Even though I had locked them up several different times before, it did not make any difference to them.

218

It was upsetting to see how Security pampered these two inmates. I would Keep-Lock them one day and the next day they were released; getting off with just a counseling session. By now this was becoming a real threat to the security in my shop. Myself; along with most of the inmates, felt very uneasy and were constantly on guard. These two inmates often bragged how they got off on misbehavior reports and had the Brass fooled when they went to the disciplinary board. I could not help but to feel a strong premonition coming over me. Something was about to happen and either Cole or Taylor would be involved in a life-threatening situation because Security would not take the misbehaver reports seriously.

CHAPTER 29

AUTHORITY SLEEPS

The system was really failing due to a lack of discipline. Each time the inmates acted up I began writing serious reports to Security and Mental Health units at the hospital. I would explain how aggressive and dangerous Cole and Taylor were becoming and needed their utmost attention. Like every other time, my reports fell on deaf ears.

When you write a Mental Health Report referral form on an inmate the report is supposed to get the inmate called into the hospital for an immediate interview where he was put through a number of tests. He is supposed to see a psychologist or a psychiatrist as well. I know Cole and Taylor had some interviews at the Mental Health unit; it was on their records. I thought if the hospital doctors were well aware of Cole and Taylor's attitudes this infraction should have been dealt with right then and there.

Security, too, is supposed to take misbehavior reports seriously and not allow them to just pile up in a corner until something happens and then act on them. Things were still looking dim. Every day I went to work I felt like this institution was sitting on a time bomb waiting to go off.

One August day, in the early morning when inmates were reporting for work, Taylor was really acting up. He refused to work and I had to lock him up, even before all the other inmates had arrived. He was becoming a real threat to security. I asked to have him removed from my class. Three days later he was released from Keep-Lock and got off with a counseling and loss of recreation for one week. That was not discipline. Inmates only got recreation once a week!

The day he returned; all the other inmates had picked up their tools and had begun working, but not Taylor. He refused to work and just sat there. I left him sitting at the table reading what looked like a small black book. When the other inmates were all set at their workstations and had all the material and tools needed I went over to the table and asked, "What is the matter now, why can't you start working?"

"My back is sore."

"Then why can't you sit at your work bench as you are sitting now and make paint brushes. I don't see the difference."

He put the book down and looked at me with killer instinct eyes and said, "If anybody ever called me a Nigger, "I'd kick their a**."

"What's this got to do with you not working?"

"It said in this book you called an inmate a Nigger."

Once again a Legal State Committee of Professionals connected with courts and the prison systems puts out this book. Any misunderstanding charges that prisoners filed against prison employees is recorded in this book, no matter if you were bought up on charges or not. Any inmate in the prison system in New

York State can acquire this book through the Law Library in the prison compound. It must be kept in their cell at all times and only be taken out when they return the book back to the law library.

I replied, "Give the book to me and I'll return it to the law library." I continued, "As for calling an inmate a Nigger that was not true. A prisoner made that remark to set me up, just like you're doing now. Case is closed! Again, give me the book." The shop was silent and you could hear a pin drop.

"You're not going to get this book, it's mine," he replied.

"I am going to write a misbehavior report on you for refusing to work, disobeying a director order and disrupting my shop."

With a smile on his face he said, "Good, that's what I wanted."

Just then the patrolling officer came in. I explained what Taylor was doing and he walked over to him and said, "Give me the book." Taylor hesitated as he looked around and then gave the book to the officer who then gave it to me. He then took Taylor to lockup.

I got my shop working again and things were quieting down. Cole seemed nervous, but kept his mouth shut.

It was now chow time and I called in the tools a little early that day to clean up. All the tools were accounted for, but the inmates were very quiet. Apparently Cole had said something to them and they were upset. As they left the shop for chow Cole waited to walk beside the officer who also leaves the shop and follows the prisoners out. Since Taylor was no longer there he was afraid that other inmates were waiting for him outside and might beat him up or shank him.

I finished writing the report and lockup for the day. I took the misbehavior report to my boss's office. He signed it, but it also needed to be signed by a Security officer, Sergeant Bulrigard. Both supervisors never challenged my report and, more importantly, neither followed through on the part where it said: *"This inmate is a real threat to security. He is always disrupting my shop and I want him removed."*

Following this last disciplinary report on Taylor he was locked up for a week. On Monday of the following week he was released and reported for roll call as usual. He got his tools and went over to his workbench. Cole also did the same. They sat next to each other talking and doing little work. I tried to ignore that. The other inmates kept their distance. The rest of the day seemed to go smoothly.

In August I was in my last week of summer vacation. Taylor came to my shop and was up to his old tricks again, being very loud and aggressive. He was pushing me to lock him up. I did not know why at the time but he got his wish. Now he could write to the Deputy Superintendent about how I was mistreating him.

Here is his letter:

In the best interest for me and security I would

like to be removed from my present program, which is "Paint Brush and Shelter work shop. I have a medical problem, a pulled muscle in my lower back. My record should show that I'm productive at my work. This problem that I have won't let me because of my physical disorder that causes severe pain. I love working, if able. My instructor, John Pecchio, has written false misbehavior reports on me. He has assassinated my character with false information to some of the inmates in the shop that I'm an informer for three Lieutenants, snitching on inmates. That alone is a threat to security and the inmates' population. John Pecchio has threatened me with a Tier-3 (Superintendent hearing). I only request that something be done about this matter. I only want to do my time in peace and would like to know why I can't.

The Deputy Superintendent must have felt sorry for this murderer-prisoner because he answered his letter the same day.

His reply was,

I received your letter. I am investigating this matter and as soon as I have sufficient information I will reply.

A copy of the inmate's letter went to the Captain of Security, Smarts, Deputy Superintendent of Programs Services, along with the Deputy's letters of recommendations. I was never informed of Taylor's intentions and threats so I was not on guard to protect myself.

To back up Taylor, Cole pushed me into locking him up and he too wrote a letter to the Superintendent in the hopes that he would add fuel to the fire and would back up Taylor's letter and make me out to be the bad guy.

On September 3 I was back on full schedule, the summer programs were over and all the instructors and teachers were back in operation. I found that Cole's letter to the Superintendent was sent back to my boss for investigation. Branch called to tell me that the "Superintendent wanted him to investigate me for writing so many Keep-Locks on inmates Cole and Taylor." I had to respond to Branch.

This approach of writing to the Superintendent by an inmate was typical. What amazes me is that Cole mentioned all the Keep-Lock I gave him and what they were for. He then asked the Superintendent "what he planned to do about it." That takes a lot of nerve. But both Cole and Taylor had a lot of that.

I sent all my reports to Branch and he responded with a letter to the Superintendent. I also attached a personal letter to the report for Branch. I told him "how appalled I was that this administration would believe such pathetic liars and troublemakers as Cole and Taylor." I had three witnesses who had signed the misbehavior reports: Ruble, the correctional officer, Security Sergeant Lepar, and Branch. Why was I being reprimanded?

Those witnesses alone should have been enough to put both inmates back in Southport prison for an attitude adjustment. Instead of writing to the superintendent, at the end of the letter I mentioned how both inmates are very argumentative, have a

225

resentful attitude toward authority and were real threats to Security. Branch never took my request seriously or bothered to reply.

That next day, September 4, Cole was out of Keep-Lock and he reported for work at about 8:20 that morning. I was issuing tools when Cole suddenly started shouting and calling me names. He wanted to be locked up again because he thought the Superintendent was on his side.

It was interesting and sad at the same time, to see how Taylor and Cole would file trumped up reports to scheme the department heads and Security when they wanted out of a program. They contradict a misbehavior report, using other inmates and staff to do it.

The responses from the department heads that read several misbehavior reports on these two inmates were devastating. They showed poor judgment, confusion and were not consistent in acknowledging life-threatening situations.

Taylor's ability to manipulate the prison's penalty system grew from the fact that he had been incarcerated ten years longer then Cole. When Taylor was ready to manipulate the system he usually began by complaining that his back hurt. It seemed that Taylor was going to remain in my shop no matter how I wrote him up. The Department's Security heads, and my boss, had ignored the misbehavior reports I wrote on Taylor, even after they had signed them admitting he was a security risk.

Well, it finally happened! On September 6, 1991, at

approximately 8:00 A.M., Taylor entered my shop and sat at the table while others worked. He kept on shouting and glaring at other inmates who wanted no part of his game. I continued passing out tools to inmates and ignored Taylor since it was obvious that he was not going to work again. When I finished passing out the tools and supplies needed I walked toward him, but before I got to him he began to curse and shout at inmates and then turned to me. I ordered him to stop, he could care less. By now I knew I could not reason with him. He was disobeying all direct orders again.

"Okay Taylor, if you're not going to work, I'll have to Keep-Lock you again!"

I did not have my radio on me because it had not yet been repaired. As I turned and continued walking toward the phone at my desk, about forty feet away, I intended to call for help. I got about ten feet away when he shouted, "Pecchio, you f***, are you man enough to challenge me?"

When I looked back at him he punched me in the face, breaking my glasses, which fell down on the concrete floor. Blood was running down my face as he continued to punch me, knocking me down to the floor. I felt dizzy and my legs became numb. I was experiencing a lot of pain all over. Still on the floor, he kept on punching me with a closed fist and kicking me anywhere he could. All I could do was try to block his blows. I pulled my knees up to my chest and crossed my arms over my face.

I could hear the other inmates shouting at Taylor. "Back off of Mr. Pecchio, leave the man alone he did nothing to you!"

That did not stop him. He continued hitting and kicking me. Then he reached down and grabbed me up off the floor, throwing me against an eight hundred pound steel stamping machine. I hit it with such force that the machine moved, forcing me down again.

I could still hear the inmates yelling at Taylor, "Leave the man alone!"

As I laid there and tried to protect myself from his blows he stopped for a second, crouching over me with both fists still clinched in a boxing stance, shouting and staring at me with mean killer eyes.

"Get up you f*****, I'll kick you're a**."

As I rolled to one side trying to get up he suddenly turned around and ran back to a table and sat down as though nothing had happened and stared at me. I laid there for a few minutes to catch my breath and then worked myself up to my desk to use the telephone to call for help. I sat down in my chair, wiping the blood from my face and waiting for help to come. The shop was very quiet and the inmates stood crowded together in the back of the shop observing everything. Just then about eight correctional officers came in full force, running in and they took over.

They asked me what had happened. As I began telling them I had my eyes on Taylor; I could hear him talking to another guard a few feet from me. He was telling him how I had attacked him first, saying he was sitting at the table minding his own business. Moments later two officers took Taylor to Keep-Lock and questioned the other inmates. A few inmates asked me if I was all right. I acknowledged them by nodding my head.

The officers took pictures of my face, broken glasses, and the machine to show how it moved when I was thrown against it. Then they took the remaining inmates back to their cells. As the inmates left I gave them the remaining doughnuts I had brought in that morning and wished them luck. I knew they would be locked up for investigation.

Branch entered the shop just as the inmates were leaving. We talked a few minutes, and then I checked my tools and locked up the cabinet. A few officers stayed in the shop and secured it. Branch then helped me as we walked to the facility hospital where I was treated. After the doctor checked me, he told me that I needed to go to an outside hospital for X-rays. Branch offered to drive me there.

The shock was wearing off and I could feel a lot more pain as we were walking toward the front entrance of the prison. When we reached the front door and were ready to leave, Superintendent Buelow was coming into the facility and stopped Branch, asking what happened. Branch did all the talking and when he finished Buelow ordered us back into the facility to see Captain Huie and to fill out the necessary papers about the incident. That was par for the course.

Buelow was more concerned about the paperwork on the

inmate than he was about me. He was apparently more concerned about protecting the state from being sued.

I was trying to fill out papers in Captain Huie's office. I was having problems communicating without my eyeglasses and because I was still shaken up from the mishap. I hurt and wanted to go to the hospital. Huie realized that my condition did not permit me to cooperate with the paperwork and offered to finish the report for me.

Halfway through the report, Huie told Branch and me that Security had been waiting to get Taylor in this position for a long time. They knew about his manipulative and hostile attitude and that he was threatening to sue the state for mistreating him physically and mentally. To secure the facility's position against any future lawsuits from Taylor they took photographs of him playing tackle football in the field house yard with other inmates. Now he was facing a new charge for assaulting an employee that would be added to his life sentences. He had been a pawn of the system.

I wished I could have punched Huie right in the nose at that point, but that was not my style. I had too much respect for authority. But in an angry voice I said, "I've been telling Security for the past thirty days how Taylor was a threat to security and requested to have him to be removed at once from my shop. Now I find out why Security was ignoring my reports, they were using me. Thanks for not listening!"

I had just finished the reports with Huie when Smarts

came in, acting very concerned. I said very little to him. Branch did all the talking. After he finished telling Smarts about the assault he left, wishing me good luck. Then Branch and I left for the hospital.

At the hospital X-rays showed no broken bones and I was told to follow up with my regular doctor because my back and legs were going numb.

Two months later, in December, while I was still home recuperating, I wrote to Commissioner Thomas Gold:

> Department heads failed to keep Central Office informed of the continuing problems employees were having with safety, especially how the prison leaders would not take employees reports seriously, jeopardizing the safety and welfare of the prison. Because of the delinquency on the part of administration leaders, I was severely assaulted by an inmate in September, making it impossible for me to continue working. I have written to you before about the seriousness of this problem and have no record of your response.
> "Respectfully yours"
> John Pecchio

I sent copies of the letter by registered mail to all of the top leaders in Central Office. The Commissioner wrote back:

> This is in response to your letter of December 4, regarding safety, security and health of employees. These issues will be addressed in an agency level decision. In your letter are the same issues that were identified in your grievance and were discussed on Friday, December 13, at the Elmira Correctional Facility. These issues will be

addressed in an agency level decision.

There was going to be a trial. The date was set in the outside court a year from now. After Taylor was sentenced by the Elmira Correctional Facility Disciplinary Board to serve one year in solitary confinement at Southport Correctional Facility for assaulting me, the sentence was somehow cut in half to six months. I called the board members and asked, "Why did Taylor only serve six months and not the full year as ordered?"

They replied, "That information is not available, and they are not at liberty to discuss it."

I reminded them that when an inmate assaults an employee he has the right to be informed of the sentence imposed on the prisoner. They then remarked, "Taylor was sent to Clinton Correctional Facility to await his trial."

I was still on compensation when the trial opened a year later. In attending the trial I was drilled for two days on the stand by Taylor's state-appointed attorney, trying to make me the bad guy.

The Assistant District Attorney, Mark Tello, was representing me. He asked the facility for my records of the attack. They came up short-handed. Somehow my reports were misplaced and could not be found. A call to Central Office requesting the same revealed very little. They faxed one page of information that should have been seven or eight.

I opened my briefcase and offered records of the assault

charges to Tello that were all signed by department heads.

"Give me what you have and I will pass it on to the judge."

About an hour later the trial resumed. There were all sorts of witnesses who testified on my behalf from the Elmira Correctional Facility: a nurse, other civilians, correctional officers, and an inmate who assisted me after the attack. When the trial ended the decision from the Jury was unanimously in my favor. Before the judge sentenced Taylor he did all he could to intimidate the jury, shouting at the judge and his attorney, using profanity, glaring at them, and saying the court was prejudiced against Blacks.

The Judge was very upset: "I will not stand for this outburst in my court room. The statements you made will be sent to the prison where you will be serving time and put into your personal folder.

"You are sentenced to three to seven years on top of your life-sentences."

This was no punishment and no discipline.

When the trial was over I left the courtroom knowing that I would not be returning to work at the prison. My department superiors had absolved themselves of any responsibility for the injuries I had received from an inmate.

My injuries and the decision, in effect, made me a victim of circumstances deliberately created by my superiors. It insured my inability to collect any monetary award from the state. They were home free with a solution to a problem they claimed I had created. The courts will not permit me a suit for a monetary settlement from the state for my physical injuries when the New York State Compensation Board has jurisdiction.

Every three to six months the Compensation Board orders me to appear before them, accompanied by my attorney, to review my case and question my state of health. The hearing lasts from ten to fifteen minutes. Doctors are called in to verify the truth contained in a documented report of my injuries. I am obliged to remain silent during these sessions and respond only when asked a question. This procedure has continued for the past ten years! Even though my medical records from State Correction and Social Security have granted me a disability status compensation doctors continue to examine me, ordered to do so by their executive board!

At the time, my case was presented to a judge in New York State. The decision later was by the presiding judge: "I find no grounds to press charges against the New York State Department of Corrections. The State Board has already granted you compensation for recognized injuries."

While working as a civilian in a prison I had first hand experience of being a victim at the mercy of a prisoner. This brutal attack on me while doing my job is a memory that will live with me for as long as I live.

CHAPTER 30

WHAT WE NEED IS DISCIPLINE

In our prisons, we have the top of the line equipment to protect the guards and civilians from prisoners with aggressive attitudes. Correctional Officers now have riot gear, including padded clothing, shields, clubs and a supervisor who leads his four to six officers into an eight by ten cell, spraying a chemical at the prisoner while all the officers wrestle the prisoner to the ground. The charge filed on this prisoner was, "The prisoner refuses to come out of his cell." I would think shutting the door of the cell, and letting him do some thinking for a long time in that cell, would solve the problem and cut medical bills for all concerned. But that would be inhumane treatment and violate the prisoner's rights! But criminals lack self-control and that is why they commit crimes.

At feeding time in some prisons, not all, where the prisoners are locked up twenty-three hours a day with one hour for recreation, the correctional officers can place themselves in a small cubicle surrounded with heavy plastic windows shaped like a dome which they wheels from cell to cell. This protects him from inmates who throw feces, urine or anything else at him while delivering their food. The only problem with this is deciding who gets to wash the machine after the correctional officer reaches a safe area and can emerge from this cubicle.

235

Prisoners are not disciplined and they are unable to become rehabilitated. They are un-confronted in their evil. Tell me the truth, are these the types of people we want back in society? Who is controlling whom?

For years now the supporters of the rehabilitation of prisoners argue that prisoners can become good citizens if given all the rights of those in a non-prison society, if they are taught a trade and if counselors, psychologists, and psychiatrists counsel them. Others believe that tougher sentences and prompt capital punishment will deter crime.

Neither approach, either alone or in combination, seems to affect the crime rate of serious and non-serious crimes in America.

On June 3, 2002, an article appeared in the *Press & Sun Bulletin*, Binghamton, NY, titled "More Ex-Cons Return to Prison Studies Show." Subtitle, "67% arrested again within three years." This article says, "More former state inmates are getting arrested again after being released from prison more than a decade ago, the Justice Department reported Sunday."

According to the article, the three-year study followed 272,211 former inmates released from prisons in fifteen states in 1994.

The percentage of re-arrest rates in relation to the crime charge is reported as follows: The general charges of larceny, stealing, and possession of stolen property are all close to 80%. What does this say about rehabilitation methods?

"Homicide, sexual assault and rape re-arrests are all between 41-46%." What does this say about programs designed to promote the safety of our families and ourselves?

The nature of recidivists is further discussed. 41% of those with only one prior arrest were re-arrested for a new crime within three years. 82% of those with more than fifteen prior arrests were re-arrested within three years.

As is always the case, reform opinions go from relaxing or abandoning the habitual criminal sentencing laws to new rehabilitation programs, to more prompt capital punishment.

I believe the oversight of prison officials and the way they manage the system should be reformed. The manipulation of the prison system by inmates should also be reformed. The manipulation of the prison system by politicians procrastinating on funding and alternately feeding and starving the prison system, should be reformed.

I believe that the inmate's self-image and respect for discipline would be learned or relearned and would be enhanced by a return to the uniformed military style drilling, common in earlier years. One article I recently read disclosed that a Japanese prison that subjected their inmates to very strict and harsh military type discipline and drilling had successfully reduced the rate of recidivism by many degrees because they learned self-discipline.

I believe that while prison officials should not indulge in the unwarranted supporting of each other against the prisoners.

The sound discipline oversight by competent leaders will eliminate the petty bickering and conniving among prison officials that is detrimental to both their welfare and the welfare of the inmates.

I believe the inmate who has acted in society without self-discipline needs to learn specifically and harshly if necessary, how to be self disciplined.

Imprisonment alone is not sufficient punishment because the prisoner escapes all responsibility for the support of himself and of his family or dependents. Some seek a return to prison for the freedom of this escape. If prisoners were forced to be productive while in prison, their earnings could then be transferred to their family and dependents. It is completely unjust that they could both escape supporting themselves while also forcing upon society the burden of supporting their dependents. Vocational and Industrial Trades gives prisoners a sense of character and responsibility and also allows them to contribute by being productive.

Our prisons should not be an escape from all self-control and discipline; it should be a return to both individual and social responsibility.

APPENDIX

PRESS CLIPPING PHOTOS

Learning a trade is good, but production of goods and services for public consumption is better because prisoners would learn to support themselves and their families. This would force them to do what many refused to do before prison, and that is to do honest, hard work to earn a living.

Vocational Shoemaking and Leather shop, as seen in 1985; with visual aids, teaching section and machines at the Elmira Correctional Facility and Reception Center.

The Modern Vocational Shoe Shop I designed over the past 25-years was rewarding to all concern. My added touch of visual aids, shoe designing, and course outline in English and Spanish help many non-English-speaking and the illiterate inmates. Later I succeeded at adding the Leather-crafts to my curriculum.

NEW YORK'S FIRST STATE PRISON
NEWGATE PRISON 1797

New York State Prison System has come a long way since
Newgate Prison, which opened on November 28, 1797.

AN IMPOSING PRESENCE IN ELMIRA, NY

This picture of the prison, taken in 1976, shows the front of the Elmira Correctional Facility, as it exists today. It sits on top of a large hill in a community located in Elmira, NY. The small building at the bottom right side of this picture replaced the Superintendent House and is now called Nine-Post. Correctional Officers stand watch here, give directions to visitors and take documents that enter and leave the facility. On top of this small building is a large siren that was set to sound off when a prison(s) escapes. (That siren is no longer in use.) The prison population averages 1700 prisoners, 450 Correctional Officers and 200 Civilians.

Cell Block in the early 1900s
Elmira Reformatory

Modern Cell Block
Elmira Correctional Facility and Reception Center
When prison behavior was a physical reality game that they could
not win and not a never-ending psychological game that nobody
wins

In the early days of New York State Prisons they used a form of discipline known as the "Shower" method (left). Prisoners were placed under the shower in a sitting position with their legs and wrists secured. They would stay in this position for hours at a time, depending on the seriousness of the crime committed in the prison compound.

In 1812, the Auburn Prison in New York State added the "Lockstep Marching Methods" (right). The prisoners stood in single file placing their left hand on each other's shoulders with their eyes looking to the right. If the prisoner stepped out of line they were quickly "Flagged" (whipped).

At this time prison leaders had complete control over the prisoners. They kept security intact, discouraged communication and instilled excellent discipline and respect in the prisoners.

When severe punishment is necessary it should have public representative oversight against abuses, but it should not be a public spectacle

Hanging was a form of execution in the earlier days of prisons. If a person was charged of criminal offenses, such as horse thieving and murder, they were hung. Large crowds would assemble outside Newgate Prison to watch the executions of men and women. In 1868 to 1901, the public executions were abolished and the prisoner was hanged inside the prison.

ATTEMPTS TO MINIMIZE THE TIME AND PAIN OF EXECUTION

New York State was the first to adopt electrocution as a method of execution. The Electric Chair was intended to replace the hanging method for serious crimes.

ANOTHER STYLE IN THE RIGHT DIRECTION

In the early 1900s the lethal gas chamber was just another form of execution. Later, new laws gave the prisoner on death row a choice in their execution—the electric chair or the gas chamber.

THE PRELIMINARY ANESTHETIC PREPARATION OF THE PRISONERS LIMITS THEIR MENTAL AND PHYSICAL TRAUMA

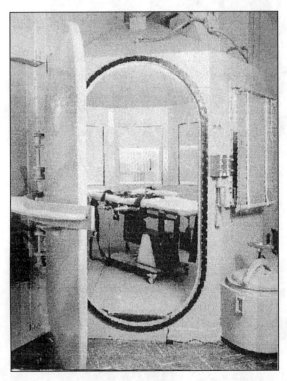

The most modern form of execution is the lethal injection chamber. This method is more humane because it puts the criminal to sleep without pain. The prisoner is strapped on a table and IVs are attached to his veins. Upon the warden's command a flow of normal saline solution is administered at a slow rate. After the sodium pentothal bromide and potassium chloride are flowing through the prisoner's veins, the physician examines the prisoner. Minutes later the execution is over. The victims suffered more pain than the criminal.

TRYOUTS FOR BASEBALL HOPEFULS

34 Area Athletes at Dunn Field In 3-Day BB Tryout Sessions

THE SKIPPER INSTRUCTS—Manager Bill Brightwell of the Elmira Pioneers (left) reviewed the procedure yesterday morning for the three-day tryout camp for baseball prospects at Dunn Field. Thirty-four athletes from the Elmira area signed for the sessions which will continue today and Friday.

BASEBALL CHAMPS

STC CHAMPS—Elmira Free Academy Saturday afternoon won the Southern Tier Conference baseball championship by defeating Johnson City 7-1 in the playoff game at Dunn Field. Team members are, front row from left, Ralph Quatrano, scorer, John Pecchio, John Myer, Jim Sampsell, Mike Stansfield, Bill Basal, John Gough, Ernie Davis and John Maher. Back row from left: Don Schreibman, manager, Pat Kane, Jim Maher, Bill Stamp, Tom Mitchell, Mike Holmes, Ed Pariso, Danny Claire, Pinky French, Chuck Prettyman, Dick Crossed, Stan Youmans, Tony Holmes and Coach Bill Wipfler. EFA won the Western Division title by edging Ithaca in a playoff Friday and came back yesterday to defeat JC and take all the marbles. EFA ended its season with a 13-5 record.

Academy Trips Southside, 6-3

By MIKE HORIGAN

Undefeated Elmira Free Academy rolled to its 11th baseball victory of the season last night by turning back Southside, 6-3, in a chilly Southern Tier Conference game at Dunn Field.

About 350 shivering fans watched Coach Bill Wipfler's boys rack up their seventh STC win and pitcher John Maher go the route for his sixth triumph.

The loss was Southside's third —all in STC play—against eight wins and just about eliminated the Hornets and the rest of the Western Division contenders for the division title as the Academy now has a three-game division lead with four conference games remaining.

This was Maher's second victory over the Hornets this season and his second STC triumph in as many days. Tuesday he won in relief at Cortland. In the first intracity clash he was a sharper as he blanked SHS, 3-0.

Little Scott Steiner, a sophomore, went the distance for Southside. He also took the loss in the first meeting of the two teams this spring.

Steiner fanned 13 batters, but was tagged solidly for 11 Academy hits. Steiner's chief nemesis was John Pecchio who banged out two singles and a double and drove in two runs.

The Academy rapped the game up in the second and third innings by scoring three in the second and adding two in the following frame to take a 5-0 lead.

Catcher Jim Sampsell opened the second by drawing Steiner's only walk. He advanced to second on a wild pitch and came home when Pecchio looped a long single to left-center.

Pecchio came all the way home when third baseman Tom McDermott threw wild to first on Mike Stansfield's grounder. The ball went into the SHS bullpen and Stansfield raced to third.

Danny Claire scored Stansfield with a sharp single to right field. Steiner settled down to get Maher on a grounder and the next two batters on strikes.

In the third Ed Pariso opened by beating out a hit to short and advanced to second on a passed ball. Chuck Prettyman singled to left scoring Pariso.

It appeared as if Steiner was out of the inning when Sampsell fanned and Prettyman was cut down trying to steal second, but Pecchio came through with a double to left-center.

Stansfield followed with a single to right and Pecchio scored EFA's fifth run.

With two out in the Hornet third, Steiner got a life on shortstop Claire's poor throw. Bill Blampied hit one to left that Stansfield dropped and Steiner came around to score. Blampied was out trying to go to third on the throw to the plate.

The longest hit of the game came in the fifth when Sampsell hit the top of the leftfield fence just inside the foul line for a triple. He scored by beating second baseman Tom Mosher's throw to the plate on Pecchio's grounder.

The Hornets picked up two in the fifth on a walk, two hits and an outfield error.

Maher had a rough time in the fourth, but escaped by fanning Marty Sweeney and Mosher to end the inning with the bases loaded.

In the junior varsity contest at Miller's Pond Field, the Little Hornets pounded out a 16-3 win over the Academy Juniors.

ACADEMY	ab	r	h	o	SOUTHSIDE	ab	r	h	o
Stamp,2b	4	0	2	1	B'mpied,ss	4	0	1	1
Holmes,cf	4	0	0	2	M'D'ott,3b	4	0	1	0
Pariso,3b	4	1	1	1	Hover,lf	4	0	2	1
P'tyman,rf	4	0	1	0	Ladd,1b	2	0	0	4
Sampsell,c	3	2	2	8	W'iting,cf	3	0	0	0
Pecchio,1b	4	2	3	7	S'eeney,rf	3	0	0	0
St'nsfield,lf	4	1	1	1	Mosher,2b	3	0	1	2
Claire,ss	3	0	1	1	Grinell,c	2	1	0	13
Maher,p	3	0	0	0	Steiner,p	3	2	1	0
Totals	33	6	11	21	Totals	28	3	6	21

```
Academy  .............. 032 010 0—6
Southside .............. 001 020 0—3
```

E—McDermott, Claire, Stamp, Stansfield, Holmes. RBI—Prettyman, Pecchio 2, Stansfield, Claire, Hover 2. 2B—Stamp, Pecchio, Hover, Steiner. 3B—Sampsell. BB—Steiner 1, Maher 1. SO—Steiner 13, Maher 8. Left—Academy 7, Southside 6. WP—Steiner. HBP—Ladd by Maher. PB—Grinnell. DP—Maher, Stamp and Pecchio; Grinnell and Mosher. W—Maher (6-0). L—Steiner (3-2). U—Antell, Callaman.

PECCHIO'S TEAM VICTORIOUS

'Many Pleasant Surprises,' Says Wipfler
EFA's 15 Baseball Victories 'Unexpected'

By AL MALLETTE

Elmira Academy failed in its bid to repeat as Southern Tier Conference baseball champ but the 15 victories compiled by the Blue Devils this season are an all-time record for a local high school baseball team.

"The number of victories was completely unexpected," commented Coach Bill Wipfler as he talked about one of the best season his EFA teams have ever enjoyed.

"I never visualized much more than a .500 season at the start. These kids simply got 'hot' and stayed that way. I think we had the better team in the championship game but you know this game of baseball . . ."

The championship game in which Wipfler refers was EFA's game with Binghamton North for the STC title. EFA waltzed to the Western Division crown while North had to battle its way through a playoff with Central

and Johnson City in the East. North kept right on battling in the title game and nipped Academy 5-4 in eight innings—ending EFA's bid for a second straight STC title and also Academy's year-long domination of STC sports.

In all EFA hung up a 15-3 record. The only teams close to EFS's 15 victories in local baseball were the 1947 SHS Hornets with a 13-0 record and this past season's Southside club with 13 victories.

Club Had Desire

What were some of the main factors in Academy's success?

"Desire and determination," answered Wipfler. "These kids had both. They played some good ball for us this season.

"There were many pleasant surprises but I think most surprising was the pitching. Who would ever have thought John Maher and Dan Johnson would win 13 games between them?

You remember Maher only won one game last year and Johnson didn't win any.

"Bill Stamp? Tremendous. But his hitting was no surprise. We saw it coming at the tailend of last season.

"And don't forget Jim Sampsell and John Pecchio. Sampsell gave us strong, steady play behind the plate and his hitting was improved 100%. Wait'll next year and watch Jim.

"Pecchio gave us a good job at first and came up with some timely hits.

"You know our infield was excellent. You don't find many better defensive high schools.

Defense Strong

"Defensively we were sound. The infield was one of the best we've had, really smooth and sharp. Claire and Stamp gave us good keystone play and with Tony Holmes in center and Sampsell behind the plate we were especially strong down the middle."

The Blue Devils lost fairly heavily through graduation in 1955, especially in pitching with Bill Basal and Dick Crossed departing. Also missing was fouryear ace Mike Holmes, Andy Mehalick, John Myer, Jim Maher and Pat Kane.

Because of these losses it came as a complete surprise to watch Academy roll through 11 straight opponents before losing its first 1956 game to Corning Academy. The 11 victories this year combined with five straight at the end of 1955 gave the Blue Devils a baseball winning streak of 16 straight—greatest victory streak in local high school baseball history.

Stamp Sets Records

Stamp set three EFA records for the season and missed out on the biggest of all by only seven points.

Stamp had 30 hits in 62 at

bats for a .484 average—tops among the EFA batters this season.

His 30 hits is a new school record—eclipsing the previous high of 25 set by Frank Gush in 1954. Stamp's other records were six doubles and 41 total bases. Mike Holmes held the previous doubles record with five and Gush the previous total base mark with 38.

The record Stamp missed by seven points was Gush's .491 batting record set in 1954.

Five other players topped .300 in batting but three veterans hit season-long slumps and ended with unusually low averages. Dan Claire hit .217, Tony Holmes .221 after a .414 season last year, and Ed Pariso .265.

Pariso, however, was one of the team's clutch hitters, driving in 16 runs. His total was second to leader Chuck Prettyman with 18.

The others over .300 were Dan Johnson .391, Bill Reed .388, Pecchio .371, Sampsell .340, Mike Stansfield .333 and Prettyman .322.

Good Nucleus Back

Wipfler has a good nucleus back next year but loses five of his top seven hitters and one of his ace pitchers.

Heading the returnees are Maher and Sampsell.

"That's a good start," says Wipfler. "I hope we'll be able to fill in behind them."

Only other regular back is Mike Stansfield. Reserves returning are catcher Bob Gush, infielder Ed Oksinski and pitchers Ernie Davis and Rusty Hood.

Wipfler figures to "fill out" with JV grads who helped Coach Marty Harrigan's club chalk up a 7-2 season record.

Most impressive of the JVs were Stan Youmans, Pinky French, Aden Galpin, Bill Freeman, Joe Long and Roy Glammichele.

BATTERY BACK—Coach Bill Wipfler will greet his ace battery back next year when baseball call goes out. From left are pitcher John Maher and catcher Jim Sampsell. Maher was 7-2 this past season.

Final Academy Averages

BATTING

	AB	H	2B	3B	HR	RBI	SB	Pct.
Bill Stamp	62	30	6	1	1	15	2	.484
Dan Johnson	23	9	0	0	1	4	0	.391
Bill Reed	18	7	0	1	0	1	1	.388
John Pecchio	62	23	2	1	1	11	0	.371
Jim Sampsell	53	18	4	3	1	11	3	.340
Mike Stansfield	30	10	0	0	0	5	0	.333
Chuck Prettyman	59	19	2	0	0	18	2	.322
Tom Mitchell	24	7	0	0	0	3	0	.291
Ed Pariso	68	18	0	2	1	16	6	.265
Tony Holmes	68	15	2	0	1	11	7	.221
John Maher	23	4	0	0	0	3	0	.174
Dan Claire	63	8	1	0	0	7	0	.127

PITCHING

	W	L	SO	BB
Dan Johnson	6	0	39	31
Lou Fossesecca	1	0	5	4
John Maher	7	2	66	29
Rusty Hood	1	1	8	15
Ernie Davis	0	0	1	6

BIG STICKERS—Two batting aces for Academy this past baseball season were Bill Stamp, left, and John Pecchio. Stamp batted .484.

254

EFA Near STC Title

Blue Devils Trip SHS for 11th Win in Row

By AL MALLETTE

Academy has knocked off its two roughest challengers in the last two days and now appears "in" as repeat champion in the Western Division of the Southern Tier Baseball Conference.

Last night at Dunn Field the Blue Devils of Coach Bill Wipfler stopped Southside 6-3 for their 11th successive victory and seventh in the STC. It followed by a day EFA's 11-inning, 5-0 shutout of Cortland.

The pair of decisions sent the Blue Devils into a three-game lead in the Western Division with only four to play. It means that Academy needs only one victory in its remaining league games with Ithaca, Cortland, Johnson City and Central to clinch at least a title tie.

Academy can get at least the tie by repeating an earlier decision over Ithaca Saturday at Ithaca.

EFA Leads Series

Academy's triumph last night put the Blue Devils into the lead by a game in the overall intracity series. The EFAs have now won 12 of the 23 games played.

There were three similarities between last night's game and the first intracity meeting 10 days before—the pitchers were the same, the final outcome was the same and it was "biting" cold. The 35-degree temperature was probably the lowest ever for an intracity baseball game, possibly the lowest ever for a local high school game.

The weather was probably a major factor in the size of the crowd last night—less than half the 750 paid for the first game May 7.

Once again John Maher outhurled Scott Steiner. But neither pitcher was as effective as in the first meeting.

Maher gained his sixth straight decision on a six-hitter. He allowed only two the first time. Loser Steiner was nicked for 11 solid base knocks last night as compared to the six he permitted in losing, 3-0, to Maher earlier.

The game itself was a bit more loosely-played—possibly because of the cold. Academy was charged with four errors and SHS one.

SHS' 3rd Loss

The loss was Southside's third in 10 games overall. Coach Bob Habersaat's Hornets are 4-3 in STC competition — same record carried by Cortland and Ithaca.

John Pecchio, with three straight line shots into left center, Jim Sampsell and Bill Stamp paced Academy at bat last night Sampsell and Stamp had two hits —one of Sampsell's a towering blast which cracked high off the left field wall and went for a triple.

Jake Hover got two of the SHS hits and gave the chilly fans a thrill in the first inning with a long shot over the left field wall which was foul by about five feet.

EFA Scores Five

Academy clinched the game in the second and third innings when five runners crossed the plate. The three second inning runs scored on a walk (only one Steiner gave), wild pitch, throwing error and two singles.

In the third an infield hit by Ed Pariso, passed ball, double by Pecchio and single by Mike Stansfield tacked two more runs on the Academy total.

The Hornets scored their first run in the third on two EFA errors. Claire's error and raced all the way home when Stansfield dropped Bill Blampied's fly in left center.

Sampsell's triple and a fielder's choice play gave EFA its final run in the fifth.

Southside's final runs scored in the fifth on a walk, outfield error of two singles.

Maher was in a bit of a jam when Steiner opened the last of the seventh with a single. But he got the next three batters to end it.

SHS Plays Friday

Southside's next game is Friday afternoon at Cortland. Ted Grinnell is expected to hurl for the Hornets. Academy plays at Ithaca Saturday with Dan Johnson pitching for EFA.

In the junior varsity game at Miller's Pond yesterday afternoon Coach Doug Wilson's Hornets pounded out a 16-3 victory over Academy—gaining revenge for an earlier loss to EFA at Parker Field.

Gene Augustine, second SHS pitcher, gained the victory. Joe Long was the loser.

Academy Dominates STC All-Star Team

Elmira Free Academy continued its dominance of Southern Tier Conference baseball by gaining three berths on the loop's all-star team but biggest surprise is the absence of pitcher John Maher from the club.

Maher, ace of the EFA pitching staff and holder of the best hurling record in the STC, got no better than honorable mention as a pair of Triple Cities hurlers, Dave Davenport of Central and Dave Patz of Johnson City, were voted to the first team.

The three Academy players named were Jim Sampsell, catcher; John Pecchio, first base; and Bill Stamp, who tied with JC's Ron Tutsky for the second base berth.

Jake Hover in left field is Southside's only nominee on the team and Bill Blampied gained honorable mention at short. Star pitcher Ted Grinnell didn't get a vote.

Only other Elmira player to gain honorable mention was Ed Pariso, EFA third baseman.

The Western Division dominated the team with seven of the spots on the 11-player team.

Others named were Jack Cummings of Ithaca, third base; Don Campos of Central, shortstop; Bill Leagens of Ithaca, centerfield; and Bob Phelps of Cortland, right field.

The three Academy choices raise to nine the number of EFA players voted to the team since it was adopted in 1953.

First were Junior Long and Frank Gush. In 1954 Mike Holmes got the nod and repeated last year. Also named last year were Tony Holmes and Bill Basal.

Tony Holmes was back with EFA this year but has not been able to hit the stride which carried him to the top last season.

SHS now has five all-stars. Previous selections were Tony Santarone, Mike Palmieri, Frank Renko and Jerry May.

The 1956 team was selected by STC coaches at the annual meeting in Candor.

1956 STC ALL-STARS

1B—John Pecchio, EFA.
2B—Bill Stamp, EFA, and Ron Tutsky, JC (Tied).
SS—Don Campos, Central.
3B—Jack Cummings, Ithaca.
LF—Jake Hover, SHS.
CF—Bill Leagens, Ithaca.
RF—Bob Phelps, Cortland.
C—Jim Sampsell, EFA.
RHP—Dave Patz, JC.
LHP—Dave Davenport, Central.

Honorable Mention—John Maher and Ed Pariso, EFA; Bill Blampied, SHS; Paul Cifonelli and Rol Rybner, Cortland; Bob Lupo, Ithaca; Bill Hallahan, Central; Craig Briggs and Bill Olcott, U-E; Dan McDevitt, North; and Bob Hill, Vestal.